The Ronald

AND OTHER PLAYS

The Ronald

AND OTHER PLAYS

CHRIS ORCUTT

The Ronald

And Other Plays
by
Chris Orcutt

First Print Edition: 2017

These plays are works of fiction. Names, characters, places and incidents either are the product of the author's imagination or are used fictitiously. Any resemblance to actual persons (living or dead), companies, institutions, villages, towns, locales or events is entirely coincidental and is not intended by the author.

High school, college and other amateur theater groups may perform any of the plays in this volume (*The Ronald* & *The Clean-Shaven Secretary with the Pistol* & *Dark and Stormy Night* & *Front Page Above the Fold* & *Microbrew* & *Kansas City This is Former Air Force One*) royalty-free; however, for professional theater companies, the plays in this volume are subject to a royalty. They are fully protected under the copyright laws of the United States, Canada, the United Kingdom, and all British Commonwealth countries, and all countries covered by the International Copyright Union, the Pan-American Copyright Convention, and the Universal Copyright Convention. All rights, including professional, amateur, motion picture, recitation, public reading, radio broadcasting, television, video or sound taping, all other forms of mechanical or electronic reproduction, such as information storage and retrieval systems and photocopying, and rights of translation into foreign languages, are strictly reserved. First-class professional applications for permission to perform any of the plays in this volume, and those other rights stated above, must be made in advance, before rehearsals begin, to the author's business manager at OrcuttWriter@gmail.com.

ISBN-13: 978-0996278362 (Have Pen, Will Travel)

Book cover image "Stock photo ID: 116688115" by Viorel Sima, used under license from Shutterstock, Inc. Cover design by Chris Orcutt. The book formatter is EBook Converting|High Quality Ebook Conversion: www.ebookconverting.com.

Also by Chris Orcutt:
A Real Piece of Work (Dakota Stevens Mystery #1)
The Rich Are Different (Dakota Stevens Mystery #2)
A Truth Stranger Than Fiction (Dakota Stevens Mystery #3)
The Perfect Triple Threat (Dakota Stevens Mystery #4)
The Man, The Myth, The Legend (Short Stories)
One Hundred Miles from Manhattan (A Novel)

www.orcutt.net

TABLE OF CONTENTS

Preface from the Author

I caught the playwriting bug in college. Although I majored in philosophy and American history, I took several Shakespeare courses and an acting class in which I adapted part of *The Great Gatsby* for a scene study assignment. Inspired when I saw the classic farce *Noises Off*, I joined a short-lived Boston improv troupe and wrote some sketches for us. I was also romantically interested in the troupe's lead actress, a driven, charismatic woman named Jules. Jules had a bale of curly black hair, glittering blue eyes, and wore red cowboy boots everywhere; I also remember her having thin eyelashes, which she tried to compensate for with copious mascara. Sadly, I can't remember her last name.

My interest in playwriting was reawakened in 2007, during a speechwriting job for Pepsi Bottling Group (PBG), when I was asked to write a play about Pepsi-Cola Inventor Caleb Bradham. The resulting Equity production, performed by Broadway actors at corporate meetings in Orlando, Florida and Scottsdale, Arizona, was a heady experience for me.

As a novelist—a person who labors in isolation for months or years, and whose only contact with my characters is seeing and hearing them in my head—I love the special magic of having my fictional creations brought to life in performance.

The morning before dress rehearsals of the Caleb Bradham play, I was sitting in a drab basement office at the PBG headquarters in Somers, New York, hunched over my laptop, making last-minute changes to the script, when a shadow appeared over me. I looked up from the computer screen, eyes blinking, and there was a beautiful woman in an Edwardian period lace dress and broad-brimmed hat. There, in the flesh, as if she had materialized off my computer screen, was my fictional creation: Caleb's fictional niece, Charlotte Bradham. She began to speak, saying her lines with a North Carolinian accent, just as I'd envisioned the character.

When she finished, the actress sat down beside me and rested her chin in her palm.

"So, what do you think, Chris?" she asked. "Am I how you imagined Charlotte?"

"No," I said. "Better."

That experience taught me a fundamental truth about playwriting: You, the playwright, might write some good dialogue, but it is the *actors*, with their mysterious gifts, that transform that dialogue from mere words on a page into living, breathing characters that make us *feel* something.

Since that experience, I've loved seeing my work performed.

Several of the plays in this collection have been performed in staged readings. *Dark and Stormy Night* & *Microbrew* & *Kansas City This is Former Air Force One* were performed by the Penobscot Theatre Company in

Bangor, Maine, during their 2011 Northern Writes New Play Festival. Thanks to the overwhelmingly positive feedback from the audience, and the encouragement of Andrew Frodahl and other festival playwrights, I continued playwriting, and in 2013, *Front Page Above the Fold* was performed by Half Moon Theatre in Poughkeepsie, New York, during the company's 10-Minute Play Festival.

Two of the plays in this collection were inspired by ideas that caught my interest and wouldn't let go. *The Clean-Shaven Secretary with the Pistol* came about when I read that Russian short story writer and playwright Anton Chekhov had written an early play with that title, but that only the title of the play survived; the text was lost shortly after the play was first performed. *Kansas City This is Former Air Force One* came to me when I saw photos of the day that Richard Nixon resigned the Presidency; he is last seen in public smiling and waving on the steps of Marine One, and I began to wonder what might have happened behind the scenes on Air Force One during his flight home from Washington, D.C.

Other plays in this collection are based on personal experience. *Dark and Stormy Night* was inspired by many late nights in my youth spent at diners in New York and Maine, flirting with waitresses. *Microbrew* is based, almost word for word, on an afternoon that my friend and I experienced with his grandmother; and before it became a play, it was a short story: "All the Young Fellas Are Linin' Up." Finally, *Front Page Above the Fold* is a spoof of my experiences writing for two Dutchess County newspapers in the early 1990s: *The Poughkeepsie Journal* and *The Millbrook Round Table*.

As for what inspired *The Ronald*, that is a story all its own.

One morning shortly after the 2016 U.S. Presidential Election, I awoke with a vision of how Donald Trump had won the Presidency. His strategy, his tactics, how he persuaded the electorate, how he gamed the media—it had all come to me in a dream. It was a miraculous moment of Gestalt.

Contrary to what many readers might think, these moments of divine inspiration are extremely rare for us writers. So, when a book (or in this case, my first full-length play) comes to us fully formed, we have to *drop everything* and write down the story unfolding within us. In my case, I've had short stories, articles and poems come to me overnight, which I wrote down in the course of a few hours, and which required very little editing afterwards; but I've never had a long work simply *given* to me the way *The Ronald* was. I didn't write it so much as it wrote itself through me; I sensed this story floating in the collective unconscious, and it chose me to draw it out of the ether and bring it to fruition.

Two weeks later, the first draft of *The Ronald* was finished. I put the play in a drawer and returned to my novel-in-progress. When I took *The Ronald* out again a month later to reread it, I found it needed very little revision. The completed play appears here almost verbatim to the version that emerged from me during those two weeks of intense writing in November 2016.

As of this writing, *The Ronald* and *The Clean-Shaven Secretary with the Pistol* have not been performed by actors, but I believe that will change. By offering royalty-free performance rights to amateur theatre companies (high schools, colleges and community theatre groups) of all of the plays in this collection, I'm hoping to make these plays—especially the political satire *The Ronald*—available to as wide an audience as possible. A portion of the proceeds from the sale of this ebook or printed book will be donated to charities. Thank you for spending your valuable leisure time with my work.

Chris Orcutt
February 2017

THE RONALD

CHARACTERS

THE RONALD: A fabulously Caucasian billionaire, reality TV star and premier luxury brand name. Sixty-something years old, perpetually impatient, wears a navy suit and glaring red tie.

HARVEY Green: Lead accountant and trusted advisor to The Ronald.

AUGUSTINA: First daughter of The Ronald and CEO of his corporate empire; early 30s, shapely and attractive; her beauty conceals her genius.

CHUCKY Cork: The younger of the two mega-billionaire Cork Brothers; actually an 1,098-year-old vampire.

DAVEY Cork: The older of the two mega-billionaire Cork Brothers; actually an 1,100-year-old vampire.

Timmy TISH: A boyishly attractive middle-aged entertainment TV reporter; long-time member of The Ronald's entourage.

LIBBY Libertine: A Liberal political reporter/pundit and debate host.

BAILEY: A fat cat Broadway producer.

FORBES: One of The Ronald's middle-aged sons.

TREASURY: One of The Ronald's middle-aged sons.

ACTOR: A young man who resembles The Ronald in his youth.

ACTRESS: A doppelgänger of Augustina, played by the same actress.

DELIVERYBOY: A young man who also resembles The Ronald in his youth.

PROFESSOR: A stereotypical rumpled, tweed jacket-wearing man in his 50s.

DINER & CAFÉ PATRONS

SHOESHINE MAN

SETTING

The Incorporated States of Freedomland.

TIME

The all-too-recent past.

Act I

SCENE— *A high-rise penthouse lair. It's a spacious room with gold accents everywhere. Along the back wall are two gold French doors to a balcony, a gold door, a gold mirror, another gold door, and a gold elevator. Outside the French doors, a city skyline gleams.*

Near the French doors, a gold telephone sits on a giant empty desk. Downstage is an indoor putting green, and a sofa and a swivel armchair facing a small platform stage.

One of the gold doors opens. Enter THE RONALD, *a man in his mid 60s with suspiciously youthful-looking and luxuriant hair, wearing a rumpled navy suit and blinding red tie. He is accompanied by a male* PROFESSOR *carrying an armload of books. The two walk to the elevator and press the button.*

PROFESSOR. An excellent session today, sir. We really covered a lot of material.

THE RONALD. We did. I especially like that idea, "It is not truth that matters, but victory."

PROFESSOR. Oh, which reminds me. [*He removes a sheet of paper from his jacket and hands it to* THE RONALD.] An item we didn't have time to discuss. Powerful ideas indeed.

THE RONALD [*puts the paper in his pocket*]. Mmm…they sure are. And ideas that will be making a comeback soon.

PROFESSOR. Excuse me, sir?

THE RONALD. Come back soon, Professor.

[*The elevator dings, the doors open.*]

PROFESSOR. Yes. Next month, correct?

THE RONALD. Yeah, sure.

[*The* PROFESSOR *steps into the elevator and exits.* THE RONALD *walks to the mirror on the wall and gazes into it.*]

THE RONALD. Mirror, mirror, on the wall…who's the best deal-maker of them all? That's right…The Ronald. [*He changes expressions and voices.*] You're fired. You're…fired. You're fi-red. You're fired? You're fired!

[*The elevator dings, the doors open. Enter* HARVEY *carrying a stack of files under one arm.*]

HARVEY. Whatcha up to, T.R.?

THE RONALD. Reminiscing, I guess. Miss that show. Miss firing people. You know, Harv, most businessmen like hiring people, like seeing that spark of hope in a man's eye. Not me. I'd rather fire 'em any day. It's a lot more fun to snuff out that spark, you know?

HARVEY. I sure do.

THE RONALD. Nothing makes a man feel more powerful than knowing he controls another man's fate.

HARVEY. That's deep, T.R., real deep. Who said that?

THE RONALD. I did. Used it in my pitch for the sequel, *The Journeyman*.

HARVEY. Have some papers for you to sign. And I've got information about those tax loopholes you asked for.

THE RONALD. Great. Sit down with me, Harv. There's something I have to discuss with you.

[THE RONALD *takes the papers from* HARVEY *and sits in his swivel chair.* HARVEY *sits on the sofa. Enter a* SHOESHINE MAN *from one of the doors, carrying a shoeshine kit. He kneels at* THE RONALD'S *feet and begins to shine his shoes, but* THE RONALD *doesn't acknowledge him. He is present through the entire act, trying to shine everyone's shoes. Every now and then, when* THE RONALD *says something stupendously offensive, the* SHOESHINE MAN *shakes his head.*]

HARVEY. What's on your mind?

THE RONALD. Did you know, Harv, in Africa, when a wildebeest is pregnant, lions will stalk it for weeks, waiting for the perfect opportunity to strike?

HARVEY. No, I didn't. Have you been watching the nature channel again, T.R.?

THE RONALD. No, I just mention that as an example. Harv, I've been stalking the political arena for forty years, waiting for the perfect opportunity to—

HARVEY. Ah…you want me to assemble a new exploratory team.

THE RONALD. Will you shut up and listen?

HARVEY. Sorry. Listening.

[THE RONALD *scrawls his signature on the papers, tosses them at* HARVEY *on the sofa, then stands and crosses to the putting green, where a putter and several golf balls sit. During the following conversation with* HARVEY, *he practices his putting.*]

THE RONALD. What was I saying? You interrupted me.

HARVEY. You've been stalking the political arena.

THE RONALD. Right. I've been stalking it from the outside, looking for weaknesses, waiting for my pregnant wildebeest. And I think it just showed up. Do I have your attention?

HARVEY. More than my attention, T.R. I'm rapt.

THE RONALD. You know who had a lot of good ideas? Hitler. Don't get me wrong, not about killing the Jews or homosexuals. That was a mistake. He committed all kinds of resources to his so-called "Final Solution," which took away from his ability to win the war. Dumb, just dumb. You don't *kill* the Jews—you keep them around to handle the money and tailor your suits. And you keep the fags around so your wives'll have somebody to go to the ballet and the opera and that gay stuff with. It's Hitler's ideas about politics and manipulating the masses that I'm talking about. He tapped right into the anger of the German people.

HARVEY. Yes, the frustration of the disenfranchised.

THE RONALD. Yeah, he tapped into the frustration of the disenfranchised and gave them someone to blame—the Jews. He created a group of "them," so he could tell the masses it was "us versus *them*." But he didn't stop there. No. He blamed the corrupt political establishment, the intellectuals, and the media. He said *they* were why Germany lost World War One. He said *they* were the reason why it took a wheelbarrow of money to buy a loaf of bread.

HARVEY. Yes, that was a very tough time. The whole world was in the grips of the Great Depression.

THE RONALD. Right, Harv. But my point is, Adolf felt the anger of the German people and he tapped into it. Well, I'm telling you, people in this country are angry. I have tremendous instincts—nobody has better instincts than I do—and they're out there…right now. They're angry and just waiting for someone to speak for them and give them a voice. And whoever does that will become the next President of the Incorporated States of Freedomland.

HARVEY. Wait a second. Are you saying The Ronald is going to run for President? I hate to break it to you, T.R., but…you don't have any political experience. I mean none. Not even a school board.

THE RONALD. That doesn't matter, Harv. In fact, right now my lack of political experience is a major asset. People are tired of the gridlock, tired of feeding and flying around those soft do-nothings, those losers. All of those Republitarian clowns, Harv. They're all *losers*. I mean look at that fat fudgeball from…what state is he from? Oh, to hell with it, doesn't matter. Point is, he's a fat loser. Looks like the before picture in a weight loss commercial. Hold on, I want to get Augustina up here.

[THE RONALD *walks over to the gold telephone on the desk and dials a number. The* SHOESHINE MAN *scrabbles after him.*]

THE RONALD [*speaking into phone*]. Get up here, Princess. And bring those new blueprints. [*He hangs up and returns to the putting green.*] They're all losers, Harv. They can't win. But I can. Know why, Harv?

HARVEY. Because you're a winner?

THE RONALD. Exactly. I'm a winner, I know how to win. And do you know how you win, Harv?

HARVEY. No, T.R. How?

THE RONALD. You lie. You lie and you keep lying, and when somebody says you're lying, you turn it around and say *they're* lying, that they're part of a conspiracy by the media. It's like Adolf said, "It is not truth that matters, but victory." Winning. The only thing that matters is winning. There'll be plenty of time for the truth once we win. But we have to win first. And to do that, we need a Big Lie, something—

HARVEY. Hold it, T.R. Remember that article about you that came out a while back?

THE RONALD. There have been so many, Harv. Which one?

HARVEY. The interview with your fifth wife, who said you kept Hitler's *Mein Kampf* and a book of his speeches by your bed?

THE RONALD. Yeah, what about it?

HARVEY. You said you didn't have those books.

THE RONALD. Nooo, Harv. What I said was, quote, "If I had those books, and I'm not saying that I do, I would never read them." Unquote.

HARVEY. But…clearly you *have* read them, T.R.

THE RONALD. No, I haven't, Harv. When you came up here earlier, did you pass a man getting off the elevator?

HARVEY. I did. Who is he?

THE RONALD. An Ivy League professor. Great guy. Hired him thirty years ago, when he was just a struggling grad student, hired him to be my personal reader. For thirty years he's been coming in once a month. He talks to me for an hour and gives me summaries of great books. Look, he gave me this.

[*He reaches in his pocket and hands* HARVEY *the slip of paper.*]

HARVEY. What is it?

THE RONALD. I don't know. Haven't read it. You read it—out loud.

HARVEY [*reading*]. A psychological profile of Adolf Hitler done by the OSS during World War Two. Quote, "His primary rules were: never allow the public to cool off; never admit a fault or wrong; never concede that there may be some good in your enemy; never leave room for alternatives; never accept blame; concentrate on one enemy at a time and blame him for everything that goes wrong; people will believe a big lie sooner than a little one; and if you repeat it frequently enough, people will sooner or later believe it." Unquote.

THE RONALD. Great stuff, great stuff. You see, Harv, I like the *ideas*. I-deahs, Harv. The ideas are great tools. What I don't like is all the fluff these writers put *around* the ideas, you know? Just give me the ideas already. I'm a busy guy, Harv, and the most valuable commodity there is, is time. And I'm running out of it.

HARVEY. Oh, don't say that, T.R. You'll be around for another…twenty years.

THE RONALD. Maybe, but one thing's for sure, even though I'm a very wealthy man with billions and billions and billions of dollars, and I have hundreds of wonderful properties and many of the finest golf courses in the world, the one thing I can't buy is time.

HARVEY. Okay, T.R., so you had some guy read these books for you—brilliant, by the way...you maintain deniability—

THE RONALD. I know.

[*The elevator dings, the doors open. Enter* AUGUSTINA, *a tall, shapely woman in her early 30s, wearing a black pencil skirt and a white silk blouse. She pauses, unbuttons her blouse until her cleavage shows, and crosses to* THE RONALD *at the putting green.*]

AUGUSTINA. Hi, Daddy.

THE RONALD [*leering into her cleavage*]. Are we *sure* you're my biological daughter?

AUGUSTINA [*giggles*]. Oh, Daddy...you always say that. Hello, Harv.

HARVEY. Hi, August.

THE RONALD. Hey, Princess...guess what?

AUGUSTINA. What, Daddy?

THE RONALD. I'm running for President.

AUGUSTINA. Oh, that's wonderful news, Daddy! Does Sapphire know?

THE RONALD. No.

HARVEY. Uh...T.R.—maybe you should discuss it with her first, so we can—

THE RONALD. Screw her. If she doesn't like it, she can go back to her one-horse village in Whogivesafuckistan. Our prenup specifically states that if I ever run for political office, she has to sit with her mouth shut and nod and smile at everything I say—no matter how sexist or racist it might be. And if she doesn't, she gets sued for breach of contract. Thank God for prenups.

AUGUSTINA. Well, I think it's terrific. You're going to be a phenomenal President, Daddy. Phenomenal.

THE RONALD. Thanks, Princess. Now take those gorgeous gams of yours over there and sit down. We'll be right over. Man talk.

[THE RONALD *slaps* AUGUSTINA *on the butt. She giggles, minces over to the sofa and sits down.*]

THE RONALD. Where were we? Before my sexy daughter got here, I mean.

HARVEY. You were starting to tell me your idea for a Big Lie.

THE RONALD. I'll get to that. You know one of the other reasons I've always been a winner, Harv? Timing. I have impeccable timing, I have the best timing. I've been stalking the political arena for forty years, and I've finally found my pregnant wildebeest. The Republitarian Party is vulnerable, Harv. They're all losers, fighting amongst themselves. Look at 'em. You've got a fat-ass loser, a guy so fat he might beat that other fat-ass for fattest President ever.

HARVEY. Taft?

THE RONALD. Yeah, whatever. You've got that schmuck from that swamp state whose brother and daddy were President. But he's a weakling, Harv. Then you've got that nut job in the House who's always quoting some "Fountainhead" book. Then you've got some little spic from the Caribbean, and another spic from Canada or something—they weren't even *born* here. Who else? Oh, that black Uncle Tom the Republitarians put on stage anytime they want to look like they're racially diverse. I hate all of them, Harv. They're all losers.

HARVEY. Then why would you want to be associated with them? The Ronald raised hundreds of thousands of dollars for them. You supported the Liberal mayor of this city years ago, and Veronica McClintock's husband when he was President. Look…if you change parties, people will think you have no loyalty. The Liberals won't trust you, and the Republitarians will think you're a RINO.

THE RONALD. RINO?

HARVEY. Republitarian In Name Only. Tell you what… why not just run as a Liberal?

THE RONALD. Because I want to win, Harv. I won't do it unless I *know* I can win, and the Liberal field is too strong. To get the nomination, I'd be up against that crackpot Socialist senator who looks like the mad scientist in the *Back to the Future* movies. And then there's Veronica—a woman, Harv. There's *no way* the liberals nominate me, not when they have a chance to support the first *woman* President ever. That's why, if I want to win, I have to join that camp of Republitarian losers and beat all of *them* first.

Harvey. And just how do you propose to do that?

The Ronald. By marketing myself as the outsider candidate. Attack them and say they're all minions of the corrupt political establishment. Sell my lack of political experience as an asset. Make them look small and don't play by any of their rules. They think the campaign's a chess match; meanwhile, I'm making it a game of jumprope. I'll say all kinds of outrageous stuff, so the media keeps putting the spotlight back on me. Are you listening, Princess?

Augustina. Of course, Daddy!

The Ronald. That's my sexy little protégé.

[The Ronald *walks to the sofa and sits down beside* Augustina, *who curls up beside him.* Harvey *paces nearby. The* Shoeshine Man *keeps trying to shine their shoes. Nobody acknowledges his presence.*]

Harvey. Hmm, it just might work, T.R.

The Ronald. I don't need you to tell me it'll work, Harv. I *know* it'll work. I understand politics, and I didn't have to spend decades in the capital swamp to do it.

Harvey. Okay, once you get the Republitarian nomination, then what?

THE RONALD. Then I win by manipulating the media. And the beauty is, Harv, we won't have to spend a penny on advertising. One thing Hitler always did is, he never let the people cool down. I've got to keep 'em angry at a group that can't hurt me—a group that's powerless.

HARVEY. Who's that?

THE RONALD. Illegal immigrants.

AUGUSTINA. Oh. My. *GOD!* It's brilliant, Daddy!

THE RONALD. I know. I'll tie in the illegal immigration with drugs and terrorism and say we need to dig a two thousand-mile moat to keep them out. Then I'll say all Muslims in this country are terrorists. And if I lose a few Muslim votes, so what? They're not in the Republitarian party anyway.

HARVEY. But what about when the media starts to attack you?

THE RONALD. That's when I attack back. I say they're all in a conspiracy against me. This'll get Republitarians even more angry. Believe me, Harv, I'll get these people whipped into a bigger frenzy than Hitler did with the Nazis at Nuremburg.

HARVEY. T.R., I wish you wouldn't draw so much from Hitler and the Nazis.

AUGUSTINA. Oh, Harv…grow a pair already.

THE RONALD. Sorry, Harv, but *ideas*, remember? They're good tools. That whole Holocaust thing was stupid of Hitler. Don't worry—it's not like I want to actually round up illegal aliens, or deport Muslims. They're just tools, Harv. They're convenient, powerless groups I can use to gain political leverage.

HARVEY. So the Big Lie is...?

THE RONALD. Something like, "The media and the political establishment have been conspiring against you for a long time, Regular Joe, so you need to vote for a total outsider: The Ronald."

HARVEY. It's great.

THE RONALD. Are you kidding? It's not great, it's *fantastic*. And I've already got my slogan, wanna hear it?

HARVEY. Of course.

THE RONALD. The Ronald for President. "Making Freedomland Fantastic Again."

HARVEY. I love it. You *are* a winner.

AUGUSTINA. You're going to make a wonderful President, Daddy! [*While kissing his cheek.*] You're going to do great, great...great...great...things!

THE RONALD. Yes I am.

[*He stands up suddenly clutching his stomach.*]

AUGUSTINA. What's wrong, Daddy?

THE RONALD. I've gotta go drop a deuce. Don't say anything good until I get back.

AUGUSTINA. We won't, Daddy. Good luck! Hope you get relief!

[*Exit* THE RONALD *through one the doors.*]

HARVEY. He's still got that constipation problem?

AUGUSTINA. Still? He's always had it. Why do you think he's frowning all the time? The man's in tremendous pain. Tremendous.

HARVEY. Running for President isn't going to help.

AUGUSTINA. I don't know. If he wins, it might trigger a *terrific* bowel movement for him. Terrific.

HARVEY. Maybe. So, how do you feel about this plan of his? Do you think he's jousting at windmills here?

AUGUSTINA. A *Don Quixote* reference, Harv? Really? How is that relevant to Daddy's running for President? I think a better reference would be the New Testament, when Jesus comes down and makes everything better. After all, Daddy *is* going to make Freedomland fantastic again.

HARVEY. My apologies. You're right.

AUGUSTINA. Time to get on board, Harv. The train's pulling out.

HARVEY. I'm on board. A hundred and ten percent.

AUGUSTINA. I'll admit though…it'll be nice to have him out of my hair so I can actually manage his empire. If nothing else, this Presidential run will keep him busy for a while. I'm really tired of him calling from the golf course during board meetings and bragging about a hole-in-one he just shot. Or him wandering around our hotel lobbies firing random employees.

HARVEY. I'm sure they're dead wood anyway. Probably need to be fired.

AUGUSTINA. But they're *not* employees most of the time, Harv—they're guests. They seem to like it, though. Always looking around for the camera, hoping they're going to be on his next show.

HARVEY. I can relate. I must have to come up here nine times a day—every time your father gets a new idea for how to hide his money.

AUGUSTINA. Well, suck it up, Harv. That's your job.

[*A toilet flushes, the door opens. Enter* THE RONALD, *frowning worse than before.*]

AUGUSTINA. Sorry, Daddy. No relief? Have you tried that imported magnesium citrate solution I got you?

THE RONALD. *Tried* it, Princess? I'm drinking it by the case. Which reminds me…I'm out of the grape flavor. Order some, would you?

AUGUSTINA [*typing on a phone*]. Done. Hmm. Are you drinking enough water?

THE RONALD. I drink water, I drink the most water.

AUGUSTINA. Well…what about vegetables? Are you getting enough roughage?

THE RONALD. I try to eat a salad every day. Look, I don't want to talk about my constipation. What do you think of my strategy?

AUGUSTINA. I think it's winning, Daddy. Winning.

THE RONALD. Harv?

HARVEY. It's a great divisive strategy for winning the election, but I have to ask you, T.R.—what would your platform be? What do you want to *do* as President?

THE RONALD. I want to make Freedomland fantastic again by using my best skill, the skill I've spent my entire career honing to a razor edge. Negotiation. I want to negotiate better deals for the Incorporated States of Freedomland. Better deals across the board. Take the Chinese.

HARVEY. Okay, what about them?

THE RONALD. Our current President's throwing those slant-eyes state *dinners*? Please. Anybody who knows anything about negotiation knows that when you have home field advantage, you leverage the hell out of it. You put bed bugs in their hotel rooms, deprive them of precious REM sleep. And as far as food goes, you don't spend a thousand bucks a plate on some fancy-ass state dinner. You keep those slant-eyes at the negotiation table day and night without sleep, and if they get faint with hunger, then, *maybe*, you send out for a bucket of chicken.

HARVEY. Hmm…they do like fried chicken over there.

THE RONALD. Everybody's ripping us off, rippin' us left and right. *Everybody*. The Chinese. The Mexicans. The Taiwanese. The Ethiopians. The Swiss. The Micronesians. The Jews in Israel. Hell, the whole Middle East. Here's another example. How about that rotten deal— that stinking un-flushed turd of a deal—that Veronica McClintock got for Freedomland with the towelheads over there? Know what I would given them, Harv? Nothing. Hell, less than nothing. I would've pulled up to the docks with a fleet of tankers and said, "Fill 'em up. And clean the windows." And when I pulled out…I would've flicked a lit cigarette off the bridge and blown up the whole friggen country.

AUGUSTINA [*laughing*]. Oh, Daddy…you're hilarious!

THE RONALD. You think so? You think I'm funny? Thanks, Princess. In the nineties, a girl reporter said I, quote, "wasn't funny." Unquote.

AUGUSTINA. How mean of her, the bitch!

THE RONALD. It's all right. I've gotten her back plenty. Every year when the list of Freedomland's 400 Richest People is published, I call her up and say, "Am I funny enough for you now?" And hang up.

AUGUSTINA. Well…you're funny enough for *me*, Daddy.

THE RONALD. Good girl. Hey, where are those blueprints?

HARVEY. Blueprints for what?

THE RONALD. My latest innovation—a luxury building with four separate but equal entrances. They can't accuse me of discrimination anymore.

AUGUSTINA. I took care of it, Daddy.

HARVEY. But…the Supreme Court overturned the doctrine of "separate but equal" a long time ago.

THE RONALD. What, Harv?

HARVEY. Nothing.

THE RONALD. Harv, order us a pizza.

HARVEY. What?

THE RONALD. A pizza.

[HARVEY *stands and crosses to the gold telephone on the desk. He dials a number.*]

HARVEY [*to* THE RONALD]. Toppings?

THE RONALD. Doesn't matter.

[THE RONALD *leans close to his daughter and speaks softly into her ear.*]

THE RONALD. Princess, I need you to keep an eye on Harv. I don't totally trust him. I need you to report back to me on everything he does and says related to my campaign.

AUGUSTINA. Of course I will, Daddy. You can trust me…a thousand percent.

THE RONALD. That's my gorgeous Princess.

HARVEY [*speaking into phone*]. Hi. I'd like to order a large, plain cheese pizza.

THE RONALD [*over his shoulder to* HARVEY]. Tell them there's a bonus if they get it here in ten minutes.

HARVEY [*speaking into phone*]. Yeah. And if you get it here in ten minutes, there'll be a bonus. The Ronald Sky Palace, penthouse. Thanks. [*He hangs up.*] They said ten minutes.

THE RONALD [*checking his watch*]. Good.

[HARVEY *returns to his seat on the sofa.*]

AUGUSTINA. Daddy, I have to get back to work. Gotta keep bringing in those billions!

THE RONALD. Good girl.

[*As* AUGUSTINA *stands,* THE RONALD *slaps her on the butt.* AUGUSTINA *giggles and minces to the elevator, where she exits.*]

THE RONALD. Anyway, where was I? Before my sexy daughter left, I mean.

HARVEY. You were talking about negotiation being part of your platform.

THE RONALD. Not *part* of my platform, Harv. That *is* my platform—negotiation, my ability to make good deals. That's it.

HARVEY. But what about problems that have nothing to do with deals?

THE RONALD. There are no problems that have nothing to do with deals. Everything's a deal.

HARVEY. All right, what about healthcare? People get sick, T.R. That's a reality you can't renegotiate.

THE RONALD. No, but we can renegotiate with the insurance companies and Big Pharma.

HARVEY. All right…infrastructure.

THE RONALD. Renegotiate.

HARVEY. Hmm…how about…our wars overseas?

THE RONALD. Renegotiate. Look, Harv, they're *all* deals, don't you see?

HARVEY. Maybe you're right.

THE RONALD. I know I'm right. We need to look at every deal we have on the table and ask, "Is this is the best interest of Freedomland?" And if it isn't, we either renegotiate for better terms, or scrap it.

HARVEY. You could be on to something here. It's nice and simple, too.

THE RONALD. Right. I'm not confusing the idiot electorate with a lot of political mumbo-jumbo.

[*The elevator dings, the doors open. Enter a pizza* DELIVERYBOY, *wearing a jacket and trucker cap with the pizzeria logo on them. He pulls a pizza box out of an insulated bag.*]

DELIVERYBOY. Large plain cheese?

THE RONALD. Come over here, son.

DELIVERYBOY. Large plain cheese?

THE RONALD. Do you know who I am?

DELIVERYBOY. Sure. You're The Ronald. Hey, would you say it to me?

THE RONALD. Say what?

DELIVERYBOY. Say, "You're fired!" Please?

THE RONALD. Maybe. Look, we changed our mind. We want a different pizza than plain cheese. What else've you got in that bag?

DELIVERYBOY. A mushroom and…an everything.

THE RONALD. Fantastic. We'll take 'em. Those and the plain.

DELIVERYBOY. I can't, sir. They're for other customers.

THE RONALD. Tell your boss I needed them. He'll understand.

DELIVERYBOY. Uh…all right. Will you be paying in cash or—

THE RONALD. I don't have any money. In fact, I need you to do me a solid.

DELIVERYBOY. What's that?

THE RONALD. I need whatever cash you have in your pocket.

DELIVERYBOY. I don't understand, sir. Aren't you one of the richest men in Freedomland?

THE RONALD. Son, I'm going to let you in on a little secret. Rich people like me don't have actual cash or liquid assets. All of my assets are in real estate—fine luxury properties around the world.

DELIVERYBOY. But how do you *pay* for stuff, sir? How do you buy food or gas or…well…anything?

THE RONALD. I don't. Businesses just give me goods and services so they can say I'm one of their customers. That's what happens when you're a wealthy celebrity like me. I think the owner of your pizzeria would like to claim me as one of his customers, don't you?

DELIVERYBOY. Yeah, probably.

THE RONALD. And wouldn't *you* like to be able to tell your friends how you did a solid for The Ronald? Gave him some pizzas, your cash, those sneakers you're wearing?

DELIVERYBOY. My sneakers? But it's cold and wet out there, sir and—

THE RONALD. You think *you're* cold? Try being homeless and shoeless. I'm on the board of a homeless shelter, son. I want to donate your sneakers. You can get another pair easily.

DELIVERYBOY. Well...since you put it like that. I might be three months behind in my rent, have seventy grand in student loans, and an expensive drug addiction, but...I guess there *are* people out there worse off than me. Okay, sure. Glad to help, sir.

THE RONALD. Good man. Leave everything on the sofa there.

[*The* DELIVERYBOY *places three pizza boxes and a wad of cash on the sofa, then removes his sneakers and puts them carefully on top.*]

DELIVERYBOY. Uh, sir? One last thing. My boss said there'd be a bonus if I got over here in ten minutes.

THE RONALD. That was nice of him.

DELIVERYBOY. No...what I mean is...he said *you'd* be paying me a bonus.

THE RONALD. If he said anything like that, he must have meant *he* would pay you a bonus. Take it up with him. [*He points at the elevator.*] Thanks for stopping by.

[*Defeated, the* DELIVERYBOY *shuffles to the elevator in his stocking feet and presses the button. The doors open.*]

THE RONALD. Hey, kid.

DELIVERYBOY. Yes, sir?

THE RONALD. You're fired!

[*Grinning, the* DELIVERYBOY *pulls out a phone and exits into the elevator. As the doors close, he speaks into the phone.*]

DELIVERYBOY [*each line decreasing in loudness*]. Dude, guess what? I met The Ronald. Yeah, and guess what else…he fired me! Yeah, way.

THE RONALD. Negotiation. See, Harv? Everything's a deal. Everything.

HARVEY. I'm sold.

[THE RONALD *goes to the pile on the sofa, pockets the cash, removes a slice of pizza and gives* HARVEY *a slice. He then picks up the pile of pizza boxes and sneakers, walks to the desk, puts down one pizza box, opens the French doors, steps outside, and throws the other two boxes and the sneakers off the balcony. When he comes back inside, he's eating the slice of pizza like nothing has happened.*]

THE RONALD. Harv, I need you to find me a [*makes air quotes*] "campaign manager." Somebody great at spin and changing the subject. I want the best. On paper, this person will "run" my campaign, but you and I know there's only one boss, and that's me. I'm going to be saying and doing a lot of crazy stuff. Sometimes it's going to seem like I've really gone batshit, but no matter what happens, don't worry—I'm just pretending.

HARVEY. Sure, but why the crazy act?

THE RONALD. Two reasons, Harv. One, because I want the media to always be paying attention to *me* and my campaign. If I'm not getting attention, I'll need to say or do something outrageous to get all eyes back on The Ronald.

HARVEY. And the second reason?

THE RONALD. To see the true character and judgment of people around me. If I'm saying and doing outrageous stuff, people on my team are going to react in two ways. The ones who go along with anything I say or do, no matter what—they either have poor judgment or they're sycophants, and I don't want either of them around when I'm President. But the ones who confront me directly about my behavior, they'll tell me the truth when I'm President, and they'll be loyal to me when things get tough.

HARVEY. But what about the campaign manager? Should he know you're just pretending to be nuts?

THE RONALD. A *she*, Harv. Make sure it's a she, and she has to be at least a seven…seven and a quarter. No dogs. I've gotta spend a lot of time around her for the next two years, and I don't want to be looking at an ugly-stick all that time. Oh…and she'll need to pitch in with the occasional bee-jay.

[*Upon hearing this, the* SHOESHINE MAN *picks up his shine box, shakes his head in disgust and exits through one of the gold doors.* THE RONALD *doesn't notice and continues his monologue.*]

THE RONALD. It's going to be unbelievably tense out there on the road, and Sapphire and Ruby aren't always going to be available. Okay?

HARVEY. Willingness to provide occasional bee-jays. Check. But should she know you're just *pretending* to be nuts?

[THE RONALD *swivels in his chair, stares across the room and spins around again.*]

THE RONALD. No. We leave her in the dark.

HARVEY. Okay, but we've got to tell August at least.

THE RONALD. Not her either. In fact, when it comes to the campaign, I don't entirely trust her. I need you to keep an eye on her, tell me what she's doing when I'm not around. *You're* the only person who'll know the truth, Harv. Tell *nobody*.

HARVEY. I'm honored to have The Ronald put so much faith in me.

THE RONALD. Yeah, yeah, whatever. Go find my [*makes air quotes*] "*campaign manager.*" And remember…at least a—

HARVEY. Seven and a quarter. Got it.

THE RONALD. No, I've changed my mind. Body can be a seven, but for the face I want…an eight.

HARVEY. Consider it done, sir.

[*He exits via the elevator. Enter, via one of the gold doors, the* SHOESHINE MAN, *who crosses to the desk, sits and eats a slice of pizza.* THE RONALD *walks to the gold mirror and speaks into it.*]

THE RONALD. Mirror, mirror, on the wall…who's the most fantastic of them all? That's right…The Ronald. [*He changes expressions and voices.*] Making Freedomland fantastic again. Fantastic again. Fan-tas-tic. Fan-*tas*-tic.

[*He gives himself a thumbs-up in the mirror and sits down in the swivel armchair. One of the gold doors opens. Enter* TISH. *He spots the pizza box on the desk and heads toward it.* THE RONALD *hears him and glances over his shoulder.*]

THE RONALD. Sit down, Timmy. I've got people coming over that I want you to meet.

TISH. Who, T.R.?

[TISH *snatches the pizza box away from the* SHOESHINE MAN, *who remains at the desk and watches the scene from there.* TISH *crosses to the sofa eating a slice, and sits down.*]

THE RONALD. The guy's just a good-looking guy. Really it's the girl I'm talking about. I've got my eye on her as a replacement for Sapphire. You know…if Sapphire lets herself go, even a little bit.

TISH. This girl…I take it she's hot.

THE RONALD. The hottest.

TISH. What's her name?

THE RONALD. Hell if I know. But she reminds me of Augustina. This girl is her spitting image.

TISH. Spitting image. Nice.

THE RONALD. We're swapping a little locker room banter here, Timmy. You okay with that?

TISH. Of course. Banterin' with The Ronald!

THE RONALD. This is totally off the record.

TISH. Chill out, T.R. There are no cameras or recorders here, and I don't have a notebook because I don't know how to write!

THE RONALD. Fantastic. I've never told anybody this— I've kind of hinted at it with August—but sometimes I fantasize about nailing her. You think that's weird?

TISH [*scoffs*]. Not at all. Your daughter's a ten, T.R.! I'm talkin' a stone-cold fox. I'd think there was something wrong with you if you *didn't* want to nail her.

THE RONALD. Glad to hear that, Timmy. You know…I don't understand why incest should be outlawed for two consenting adults. I mean, if your daughter's a grown woman and is into it, and you use protection.

TISH. Don't want any three-headed babies.

THE RONALD. That's for sure. Anyway, wait till you see this girl. She's going to be all over me like a gay tuxedo salesman.

TISH. Can't wait.

THE RONALD. You know, Timmy, when you're a wealthy celebrity like me, girls'll let you do anything. I've walked right up to them and grabbed 'em right by the crotch.

TISH. Really?

THE RONALD. Sure. Like I'm holding up a bowling ball.

TISH. Whoa…The Ronald!

THE RONALD. But you know what they like most? And they *all* like this. I picked it up from President Mc-Clintock at a fundraiser for him twenty-five years ago. They love it when you shake their hand gently and hold their upper arm with your other hand. Then, when you're about to finish the handshake, you give their breast a good squeeze. I mean get right in there and take a *bite*, you know?

TISH. Really?

THE RONALD. Oh, they love it. They *all* love it. You'll see.

[*The elevator dings, the doors open. Enter* BAILEY, *the quintessential fat-cat Broadway producer with an unlit cigar in his mouth, followed by an* ACTOR *and* ACTRESS. *The* ACTOR *is extremely handsome; he has a thick head of hair and wears a navy suit with a red tie like* THE RONALD's. *He is obviously a younger, idealized version of* THE RONALD. *The* ACTRESS, *the doppelgänger of Augustina, has a shapely figure and wears the same black pencil skirt and white blouse as Augustina. From the moment she walks in, the* ACTRESS *winks at and flirts with* THE RONALD.]

ACTRESS. *Hi*, T.R.

THE RONALD. Hi.

ACTOR. It's a pleasure to be rehearsing for you again, sir. Thank you again for this oppor—

THE RONALD. Yeah, yeah. Whaddaya got for me today, Bailey?

BAILEY. A revised scene from the show. That is, unless you'd like them to do a few show tunes.

TISH [*raising his hand*]. Excuse me...question for The Ronald. [*Turns to him.*] Show tunes?

The Ronald. I love musicals, but I hate the theaters. The seats are a complete rip-off, and everybody's coughing and sneezing. So I have these kids come over sometimes and give me private shows. Numbers from *Oklahoma, Annie Get Your Gun, The Producers*—you name it. And if I get bored with a number, I just say, "Bor-ing! Next!"

Tish. Awesome. Your very own Broadway remote control.

The Ronald. Exactly. Bailey...not tonight. But I'd like the girl to come back tomorrow—in costume—and do a few numbers from *Chicago*.

Bailey [*glancing at the* Actress]. I'm sure that can be arranged.

Actress. It certainly can. *Anything* for The Ronald.

[The Ronald *nudges* Tish, *then snaps his fingers like a wheeler-dealer.*]

The Ronald. Okay, Bailey, I'm busy. Gotta go, gotta go.

Tish. What are they performing?

The Ronald. It's from the play Bailey's producing about my life. It's called...*The Ronald.*

Tish. I like it.

The Ronald. Shut up, Timmy. I don't care if you like it. Go, Bailey. Let's do this thing.

BAILEY [*sitting in the armchair*]. All right, guys…like we rehearsed last night, from the top. The scene is on a Midtown rooftop. Our lovers gaze across the city.

[*The* ACTOR *and* ACTRESS *step onto the platform stage, lightly embrace and gaze across the room into the distance.*]

ACTRESS. I can't believe it's all yours. This whole, great big, glorious city. And to think…you started with nothing but your wits and an itty-bitty million-dollar loan from your father.

ACTOR. I know. And he even charged me interest—one over prime.

ACTRESS. What worlds does The Ronald have left to conquer? What's left out there that he doesn't own yet?

ACTOR. You.

ACTRESS. Well…I won't come cheap.

ACTOR. I don't care. I've bought expensive properties before. And they always appreciate in value.

ACTRESS. Really?

ACTOR. Always.

ACTRESS. But my father's against us. He's threatened to buy an island and imprison me on it if I keep seeing you.

ACTOR. Then I'll buy the island next door, build a luxury resort on it, sail over and rescue you.

ACTRESS. You'd do that for me?

ACTOR. To hell with your father. He's a loser. I'm a winner. Marry me. Marry me and become the most beautiful property in my portfolio.

ACTRESS. So romantic. Okay…I'll do it.

ACTOR. Fantastic. Hey, now that that's settled…let's have sex up here. I like the danger of falling off the roof.

ACTRESS. Yeah, I'm freaky like that, too. I'll let you dangle me off the edge, darling.

ACTOR. All right, let's do this thing.

[*The* ACTOR *and* ACTRESS *stop and look at* THE RONALD. TISH *claps furiously.*]

BAILEY [*sitting up*]. So…any notes, T.R.?

THE RONALD. I like the changes. I like where he says, "Marry me and become the most beautiful property in my portfolio." I actually used that line on my fourth wife—Augustina's mother. All right, Bailey. You and younger me and can beat it. I want to talk to the girl for a minute.

[*Exit* BAILEY *and the* ACTOR *via the elevator.* THE RONALD *stands and shakes the* ACTRESS' *hand—the way he described to* TISH.]

THE RONALD. And you, my dear, are what we in the business call an undervalued luxury property.

ACTRESS. I am?

TISH [to ACTRESS]. Hey, honey, this is The Ronald! Give him a little hug, huh?

[As *the* ACTRESS *leans in to hug him,* THE RONALD *scoots his hand across her arm, grabs her breast and gives it a honk.*]

ACTRESS. Hey!

THE RONALD. What's wrong?

ACTRESS. You just grabbed my breast!

THE RONALD. No I didn't.

ACTRESS. Yes you did.

THE RONALD. Timmy, did I grab her breast?

TISH. Of course not. You're The Ronald!

ACTRESS. This is such bullshit.

[*She storms over to the elevator and punches the button.*]

THE RONALD. So I'll see you tomorrow night.

ACTRESS. For what?

THE RONALD. The private show. Remember, it's *Chicago*, so wear lingerie. I like black. And bone up on some numbers from *How to Succeed in Business Without Really Trying*. Tell you what…I want you to combine the two shows and do a little strip show medley for me.

ACTRESS. You must be insane. I'm not coming back tomorrow.

THE RONALD. Oh, grow up, honey. Do you want to star in your first Broadway show or not?

ACTRESS. Yes.

THE RONALD. Then suck it up and be back here tomorrow night.

[*The elevator dings, the doors open, and the* ACTRESS *exits.* TISH *holds up a fist, and he and* THE RONALD *do a fist-bump and "blow it up."*]

TISH. The Ronald does it again!

THE RONALD. Of course I did. I always get what I want. I win, Timmy. That's what I do.

TISH. But she didn't seem to like the move that much.

THE RONALD. No, she did. She just acted like that to cover for herself. No girl wants a guy thinking she's easy.

TISH. Mmm, makes sense.

THE RONALD. Of course it does. I know women, I have the best insight into women. Women love me. But did you notice my negotiation skills in that situation? Because the way I renegotiated there was really something to see. They ought to invite me back to my Ivy League school to teach a master class in this stuff.

TISH. What do you mean?

THE RONALD. All right, I don't have a lot of time, so listen carefully.

TISH. Learnin' negotiation skills with The Ronald! Ready.

THE RONALD. Normally if somebody gets caught [*makes air quotes*] "in the wrong," he'll concede on a point. He'll say, "Okay, honey, I apologize. That was wrong of me. I understand your discomfort and why you don't want to come back tomorrow night."

TISH. But you didn't do that.

THE RONALD. Correct. I didn't concede on any point. In fact, since I knew I had terrific *leverage*—her desire to keep her acting job—I upped the ante. I tacked on *new* terms to sweeten the deal for myself. Now she'll be doing a number from a second show *and* wearing the outfit I described.

TISH. So that's not sexual harassment, right?

[THE RONALD *flaps his hands dismissively.*]

THE RONALD. *Please.* A term invented by politically correct pantywaists. What you saw there was a deal like any other deal. It was a transaction between a man and a woman, and the man got the better end of it. Women need to stop their bitching and moaning and accept the fact that men were given testosterone.

TISH. You really are amazing, T.R. Wanna hang today?

The Ronald. Can't. Got work to do. Why, what are you up to?

Tish. Well, remember those [*makes air quotes*] "blood drives" we used to do with the network's Winnebago?

The Ronald. No. Remind me.

Tish. Oh, it's classic. Me and some buddies dress up like doctors, go to college campuses and say we only want girl blood. Then, when the girls get in the Winnebago, we say they have to give their blood topless. You know…so it's *sanitary*.

The Ronald. Ah, now I remember. Good times. Wish I could join you, Timmy, I really do. You can do it 'cause nobody knows who the hell you are. But I'm too wealthy and famous now. They'd spot me in a second.

Tish. Come on, it'll be great! We'll give you a fake mustache.

The Ronald. Sorry, pal. Can't.

Tish. All right. Later.

[Tish *exits via the elevator.* The Ronald *stands and crosses to the putting green, where he attempts a very long putt and speaks in a soft, golf announcer's voice.*]

The Ronald. The Ronald is the only billionaire to become President of Freedomland. And now, ladies and gentlemen, if he makes this putt, he'll be the first President to win the British Open.

[*He taps the putt, and the ball misses by inches. Even though* THE RONALD *is alone, he looks around anyway to make sure no one is watching, then he nudges the ball into the hole.*]

THE RONALD. He does it! The crowd goes wild!

[*The elevator dings, the doors open. Enter the Cork Brothers,* CHUCKY *and* DAVEY. *They frequently interrupt each other and complete each other's sentences. They are pale-complexioned, wear old-fashioned fedoras and trench coats with the collars up. One of them struggles with a giant, dusty book that looks like a book of witch's spells. He carries it to the desk and drops it with a heavy thud.* THE RONALD *hasn't seen them yet.*]

THE RONALD. Hey, Timmy…I just drained a thirty-footer. It was a beautiful thing to see. [*Turning, he sees the Cork Brothers.*] Who are you guys?

CHUCKY. The Cork Brothers. I'm Chucky, and this is Davey.

THE RONALD. Interesting. I always thought you guys were a myth. Like the Freemasons, or female orgasms.

CHUCKY. No we're—

DAVEY. Quite real. We wanted to pay you a visit and express our support. See if—

CHUCKY. You needed anything in the way of resources.

THE RONALD. Support for what?

DAVEY. Your Presidential run.

THE RONALD. How do you know about that? Only my daughter Augustina and Harv—

CHUCKY. Let's put it this way…we—

DAVEY. Have people everywhere.

CHUCKY. Question. How would The Ronald like unlimited financial resources for his campaign?

THE RONALD. I don't need your money. I'm a very, very, very wealthy man, and I plan on financing my campaign myself. I'm not going to have you guys or any other rich schmucks owning The Ronald.

CHUCKY. Well, what kind of money are we talking about?

THE RONALD. Excuse me?

DAVEY. How much are you worth?

THE RONALD. None of your business.

CHUCKY. Because my brother and I suspect you live a rich man's lifestyle—

DAVEY. While you're actually in heavy debt.

CHUCKY. You've declared bankruptcy several times. I think you're a debtor.

THE RONALD. I'm not a debtor, you're the debtor.

DAVEY. I don't think so. We—

CHUCKY. Own Canada.

THE RONALD. What?

CHUCKY. We own—

DAVEY. Canada.

CHUCKY. Own all the land. Owned it for almost a thousand years—and we rent it to the Canadians.

DAVEY. The people and the government.

CHUCKY. They're good people up there.

DAVEY. Freedomland's hat!

THE RONALD. You *own* Canada? You must be worth *trillions*.

DAVEY [*glances at a pocket watch*]. Chucky, we need to get a move on. Tick-tock.

CHUCKY. Right. Hey, T.R., come over to the window with me. I want you to see something.

[THE RONALD *walks over to the French doors, where* CHUCKY *puts an arm over his shoulder.*]

CHUCKY. Join with us, and you'll have everything, for as far as you can see. All you have to do is take our money and do us a few favors once you're President.

THE RONALD. Favors? Like what?

DAVEY. Like put judges on the Supreme Court who will guarantee the rights of corporations. Hell, to our mind, corporations are more interesting than most humans. And—

CHUCKY. You can never sign any treaties on global warming, or climate change, or—

DAVEY. Whatever those annoying pointy-heads are calling it this week. Even though it's a total crock.

CHUCKY. *And* you have to keep de-funding public education.

THE RONALD. Why's that?

DAVEY. Because education is the silver bullet, and we need the electorate as ignorant as possible. We need them to be constantly fighting between themselves, which is why—

CHUCKY. You have to maintain the illusion there's a big difference between the Republitarians and the Liberals.

THE RONALD. I have plenty of money for my own campaign so—

CHUCKY. We'll give you a billion dollars. And whatever you don't spend—

DAVEY. Is yours to keep.

CHUCKY. Look, Ronnie…we know what we're doing. We've been at this for quite a while.

DAVEY. Nine hundred years, give or take fifty.

CHUCKY. Heck, we *invented* lobbyists.

THE RONALD. What?

DAVEY. Sure, it was 1801 and we were having trouble with the Democratic-Republicans in Congress, so we—

CHUCKY. Sent a few guys down to the Capitol with simple instructions.

DAVEY. Go hang out in the lobby and throw money on the floor.

CHUCKY. Ah…seeing those senators scrabbling around for dimes. [*Nudges* DAVEY.] Wasn't that hilarious?

DAVEY. Sure was. [*To* THE RONALD.] We're great judges of political horseflesh, and you, young man—

CHUCKY. Are the most promising horse we've seen since Joey or Adolf.

THE RONALD. Joey?

CHUCKY. Joseph Stalin.

DAVEY. We backed both of them.

CHUCKY. After eight centuries, we learned the hard way.

DAVEY. You've got to—

CHUCKY. Cover your bets.

DAVEY. We also backed…let's see…Napoleon, Ivan the Terrible, Henry the Eighth—

CHUCKY. Genghis Khan. Don't forget Genghis.

DAVEY. How could I forget *him*, Chucky? Talk about *charisma*.

THE RONALD. Wait a second…how old are you guys?

CHUCKY. Well, I'm the baby. I'm one thousand ninety-eight.

DAVEY. And I'm eleven hundred.

CHUCKY. We're vampires, T.R.

THE RONALD. Okay.

CHUCKY. You don't seem surprised.

DAVEY [*to* CHUCKY]. Tick-tock, Chucky.

CHUCKY. Right, right. The thing is, T.R., we're hoping you're a T.R. we can work with. The original one—

DAVEY. Theodore Roosevelt—

CHUCKY. Was a bully. Took over the Presidency when our hand-picked guy, McKinley, was assassinated. When we dropped in on T.R. to buy him, he—

DAVEY [*rubs his jaw*]. Punched me in the mouth and called us, quote, "malefactors of great wealth," "tremulous troglodytes," and…what was that other thing? Remember? We had to look it up.

CHUCKY. "Ridiculous ridglings."

THE RONALD. What the hell is a ridgling?

CHUCKY. A colt whose balls haven't dropped yet.

DAVEY. Be that as it may…we need to know if you're somebody we can work with.

CHUCKY. Oh, Davey, tell him about the other thing.

DAVEY. What other thing?

CHUCKY. The social media thing. The tie-in. You know…

DAVEY. *Yessssss.* We're trying something new in this election cycle, T.R., and there's a sweet little hundred-million-dollar bonus for you if you'll play along.

THE RONALD. I already have a hundred million, but I'll take another. What do I have to do?

CHUCKY. You know we own the social media platforms Facetwit and Twitbook, right?

DAVEY. Chucky…of course he does. The Ronald's been shooting his mouth off on them every ten minutes for a decade.

CHUCKY. Duh. Well…all you have to do is keep shooting your mouth off about whatever you want—

THE RONALD. That was already my plan.

DAVEY. Meanwhile, Chucky and I will be doing something new, something we're calling "fake news."

CHUCKY. Just making up news stories about things that aren't true, planting them in social media, and letting the rabble fight over them.

DAVEY. Thus creating a tidy distraction that gets them arguing about things that don't matter—

CHUCKY. And not directing their anger at us one-percenters. It turns out there's already a news network with a lot of experience in fake news—POX News—so we just hired a bunch of their "journalists."

DAVEY. You see, T.R., it's imperative that the populace *not* start talking about the real issue—the thing that really keeps all of them down, and that's—

CHUCKY. Income inequality. We had a scare some years back with that hashtag-occupy movement, and recently that former labor secretary—

DAVEY. That guy that looks like the Mayor of Munchkinland—

CHUCKY. He's started talking about it again. The problem is, he's brilliant and a great teacher, and Davey and I are afraid he might actually be getting *through* to people this time.

DAVEY. Which is why you are *never* to release your tax information, by the way.

CHUCKY. Yeah, we've seen your filings, and we know you haven't paid shit in Federal income tax—ever. It's impressive.

THE RONALD. Thanks. A lot of the credit goes to my lead accountant, Harvey Green, but—

DAVEY. You see, Chucky and I were behind those revisions of the tax code in 1969 and '86, when we got the tax rate of the highest bracket reduced from—

CHUCKY. Ninety percent to thirty-nine.

DAVEY. In the years since, we've also gotten reductions in capital gains taxes, too, but our goal for your administration—

CHUCKY. Is for the top one-percent to pay *nothing* in taxes. Nothing. Not even car registration fees.

THE RONALD. I couldn't agree more. We shouldn't be paying a damn thing. We're the wealthy. We're the winners. We're what make this country fantastic. The great unwashed should be kissing our feet that we choose to live here and grace this country with our presence. What are our taxes being spent on anyway? All stuff that doesn't benefit us. Social Security? Medicaid? Screw you—I don't have to worry about my retirement or medical care. The military? That's what the poor are for—to be soldiers. The only thing we currently use are roads and bridges, but as soon as we get our flying cars—cars that only us rich will be able to afford—we can fly right over that problem. On the maiden flight of *my* flying car, I plan on dropping a deuce onto a low-income housing project. I can't wait.

DAVEY. We like your vision, T.R. Clearly you're a guy we can work with.

CHUCKY. And after the election, we'll come back and give you the opportunity to become one of us.

THE RONALD. What do you mean?

CHUCKY. We'll make you a fellow vampire. Undead. Eternal life.

THE RONALD. Hmm. Question about that. Would my johnson still work?

DAVEY. Johnson?

THE RONALD. My phallus. My dong. My rod. My schlong.

CHUCKY. Mmm…probably not. Mine hasn't since…the Middle Ages.

THE RONALD [*winces*] . Oh. Well, I'll have to think about it. By the way…what's that giant book?

[*The three of them walk over to the desk.* DAVEY *opens it and leafs through the pages.*]

DAVEY. Ah…*this* is our political playbook.

CHUCKY. Chock full of nine hundred years of political dirty tricks.

DAVEY. Some of the handwriting's hard to read because it goes back a long way, but there's a lot of recent stuff in here, too.

CHUCKY. Nixon added a couple of good ones, along with Lee Atwater—

DAVEY. But the best recent additions were by Karl Rove. Talk about an incredible sawed-off evil genius. The guy's such a douchebag, even *we* don't like him.

CHUCKY. Anyway, T.R., you should feel free to flip through it, use a few ideas, and add a few of your own. But don't spill coffee on it or anything. It's our only copy.

THE RONALD. Yeah, sure. Now, about the money. One-point-one billion, correct?

DAVEY. Correct. We usually put it in a Caymans account. Does that work for you?

THE RONALD. That's fine.

CHUCKY. Good, because we own the Cayman Islands, too.

DAVEY [*checks his watch*]. Chucky, we've gotta move. Sunrise is in thirty minutes.

[*The brothers run to the elevator and hit the button. The doors open.*]

THE RONALD. Wait…what happens at sunrise?

CHUCKY. The sun burns our flesh off. Sorry, T.R. Gotta run. Stay in touch. Bye.

[*The brothers step aboard and exit.* THE RONALD *crosses to the gold telephone and makes a call.*]

THE RONALD [*into phone*]. Get everybody up here. We're announcing. [*He hangs up, walks to the gold mirror, and speaks into it.*] Making Freedomland fantastic again. Fan-tas-tic. Fan-*tas*-tic.

[*The elevator dings, the doors open. Enter* HARVEY, *the* PROFESSOR, BAILEY, *and* TISH. *Last to enter are* THE RONALD'*s sons,* FORBES *and* TREASURY. *The two sons wear old-fashioned football sweaters with the letters "T.R.U." on the front. They remain standing, tossing a football around, while the others either sit on the sofa or stand nearby.*]

FORBES. Hey, Pop! What's going on? Wanna see some of the moves me and Treasury have been workin' on?

TREASURY. Yeah, Pop! Check out this one! I call it the old twenty-four-karat skidoo!

[*Clutching the football against his chest,* TREASURY *runs rampant around the stage, plowing into other characters, diving over the sofa, and exiting through one of the gold doors. Enter via the other gold door the* SHOESHINE MAN, *who sits alone at the desk upstage.* THE RONALD *sits in his swivel chair.*]

THE RONALD. I'm glad you're all here. Wait…where's Augustina?

[*The elevator dings, the doors open. Enter* AUGUSTINA. *She unbuttons her blouse, walks over to the swivel chair and sits on* THE RONALD'*s lap.*]

AUGUSTINA. Sorry I'm late, Daddy. Been dealing with a crisis. Some *idiot* threw pizza off our building, and it landed on one of the guests.

THE RONALD. Wasn't me. I didn't do it.

AUGUSTINA. Did you tell everyone yet?

TISH. Tell us what?

THE RONALD. Everyone, I want to make an announcement. The Ronald is running for President of the Incorporated States of Freedomland.

[*Everyone claps, hoots and whistles. Enter* TREASURY, *via the gold door again.*]

THE RONALD. The reason I've called you all together is because you're all going to be playing a role on my team. Professor, you're my idea man. I want nothing but the best ideas for my campaign.

PROFESSOR. Certainly, sir.

THE RONALD. Harv, you're in charge of the money. We'll be telling the voters that since I'm a very, very, very wealthy man, I'll be paying for my campaign myself. But…guess what?

HARVEY. We're not?

THE RONALD. Correct. We've got cash coming in from a secret source, but I want more. Let's solicit donations online. Appeal to middle- and low-income voters to send us their last dollar. Maybe start a national campaign encouraging kids to donate their milk money.

HARVEY. Understood, sir.

THE RONALD. Bailey, you're producing my rallies. I want the craziest crazies at my rallies. I want you to stage fights and protests to keep the TV cameras on me all the time.

BAILEY. You got it, T.R.

THE RONALD. Boys?

FORBES. Yeah, Pop?

TREASURY. Yeah, Pop?

THE RONALD. Your job is to wear a couple of smart Brooks Brothers suits and nod at everything I say, as if it's the most amazing thing you've ever heard. Otherwise, you keep your annoyingly small caviar holes *shut* and let Augustina do the talking. Is that clear?

TREASURY. Sure, Pop!

FORBES. Sure, Pop!

TISH. What's my job?

THE RONALD. The over-fifty, drinking at eleven a.m. set finds you pretty cute. Your job is to go on the morning talk shows and kiss their cellulite asses for me.

TISH. Kissin' ass for The Ronald! You bet!

FORBES. What's Augustina's job?

TREASURY. Yeah, what's she doing?

THE RONALD. She knows. Here's the deal. You're all competing for a job in my Presidential administration. Only one of you will be coming with me to our nation's capital, where you'll be given a job with tremendous power and a *yooooge* salary. And the rest of you…will be fired. Okay, questions? No?

[*He slaps* AUGUSTINA *on her butt; she giggles and the two of them stand.* AUGUSTINA *straightens his tie.*]

THE RONALD. All right. Let's do this thing.

[*Exeunt into the elevator everyone but the* SHOESHINE MAN. *The doors close.*]

CURTAIN

Act II

SCENE— *The high-rise penthouse lair, with a couple of set changes. Atop the small platform stage is now a lectern, angled toward the living area and the audience. Downstage, between the lectern and the audience, is a table with two rolling chairs. A network logo (LBN) hangs from the table. This is where the reporter/debate host* LIBBY *Libertine sits; she faces the audience when she's reporting, and sits in quarter-profile to the audience when she's hosting a debate. Downstage opposite, the putting green has been replaced by a diner booth with two* DINER PATRONS. *Seated behind the table,* LIBBY *Libertine wears black horn-rimmed glasses and mugs to the audience. A self-important "news theme" plays loudly overhead for a few seconds and fades out.*

LIBBY. Good evening and welcome to another edition of the Liberal News Hour on LBN, with me, Libby Libertine, your smart-alecky, acceptably militant, Liberal lesbian host! Liberals and Republitarians, hold on tight! The Ronald is running for President. Yes, you heard that right. The Ronald—the internationally famous billionaire, reality TV star, and hairdo—is…running…for…President. Now, before I go any further, might I interject at this juncture just how *insane* this is? I mean, *what* is the Republitarian party thinking? Hello, RNC? *Hello?!* Seriously…you guys would be better off putting a New York pretzel vendor on the ticket. But maybe, folks, I should be thanking them. Most of the time my job is to snipe at the Republitarians from the safety of the sidelines.

But with The Ronald in the race, I'm finally going to get to use my political rant power-sprayer! I loathe this man and everything he stands for, but let's face it… he's great for ratings! Back to the Republitarians in a moment. Let's take a look at the Liberal field, with its *fabulous* woman front-runner, Veronica McClintock. Smugedy-smug-smug, *lorem ipsum liberalum intelligentsium superioridum.* We'll talk about all of this and more…after the break!

[*Enter* THE RONALD *and* HARVEY *via one of the gold doors. They sit on the sofa together.* HARVEY *is relaxed with his legs crossed, but* THE RONALD *is clearly agitated. The* SHOESHINE MAN *walks over and shines their shoes.*]

THE RONALD. I'm bored, Harv. We announced, did a couple of speeches, and now what? Nothing. This sucks.

HARVEY. This is the dead time in campaigns, T.R. We haven't gotten to the Republitarian debates or the primaries yet.

THE RONALD. But the media isn't paying attention to me, Harv. I'm getting zero attention, and it's making me really uncomfortable.

HARVEY. They're not paying attention to *any* of the candidates right now. There's nothing to report.

THE RONALD. Oh yeah? Report *this.*

[*He pulls out a smartphone and speaks aloud as he types.*]

THE RONALD. Freedomland…hey, Harv?

HARVEY. Sir?

THE RONALD. The super-erect dong thingy on here—what's that called again?

HARVEY. An exclamation point?

THE RONALD. Yeah, exclamation point. Freedomland! Exclamation point. The terrorists are coming across our southern border. If I'm Prez, we'll dig a two-thousand mile moat and make the spics pay for it! Exclamation point. LMFAO! Exclamation point. And... *send* that baby! Now, Harv...watch the fun. This is gonna be hilarious.

[*The* DINER PATRONS *stare at smartphones as they sip coffee.*]

DINER PATRON #1. Wow, didya read The Ronald's latest Facetwit? He's gonna dig a moat on our southern border and make the spics pay for it. I love this guy! 'Bout time somebody stood up to them.

DINER PATRON #2. I know. No politically correct BS for this guy.

DINER PATRON #1. Haven't I been saying this for *years*? That we need a moat down there? Huh?

DINER PATRON #2. You have. Uh-oh...the spic President just replied. Says they're not gonna pay.

[THE RONALD *is still hunched over his smartphone.*]

THE RONALD. He just replied.

HARVEY. Who just replied?

THE RONALD. President of Mexico. Says they won't be paying for our moat. [*He speaks aloud as he starts typing.*] You know what, Julio? The moat just got a hundred feet wider, and I'm personally going to kidnap your ass and put you on the chain gang that digs it! Exclamation point. See you in two years! Exclamation point. And...send. Come on, Harv, let's hit the peep shows on Eighth Avenue. My treat. I've got my lifetime VIP card.

[*Exeunt* THE RONALD *and* HARVEY *via the elevator. At her table,* LIBBY *is beside herself with excitement. The "news theme" plays and fades out quickly.*]

LIBBY. *Well*...today Republitarian Presidential candidate The Ronald dropped a social media A-bomb on Mexico, declaring on Facetwit that if elected President, he would dig a two-thousand mile moat between our two countries. *And* if that weren't bad enough, he threatened to kidnap the President of Mexico and put him on the chain gang to dig the moat! Folks, this is sheer insanity! Will somebody on The Ronald's campaign *please* talk to this man before he starts World War Three?

[*Enter* TISH *via one of the gold doors. Simultaneously, the elevator dings, the doors open.* AUGUSTINA *enters, unbuttoning her blouse.*]

AUGUSTINA. Timmy, where's my father?

TISH. The Ronald? No idea. I've been interviewing at a red carpet all night. Just popped in for some hair gel and a box of roofies.

AUGUSTINA. I'm glad you're here. I want to talk with you.

TISH. Yeah, August? I want to do more than *talk* with you.

[TISH *reaches for one of her blouse lapels.* AUGUSTINA *swats his hand away.*]

AUGUSTINA. Never going to happen. Look, I know that back in the day you and my father did some wild things together. Judging those Spring Break bikini contests, posing as porn producers, co-authoring that dinosaur erotica series...

TISH. Those are just the tip of the iceberg, August.

AUGUSTINA. Whatever. Do you know about these Facetwit posts he's been making? You'd better not be encouraging him.

TISH. The moat? No I didn't know. But it's pretty cool. Your Dad's awesome.

AUGUSTINA. Shut up. Your job is to work the morning talk shows and stick to the script. Here's the bottom line, moron—stay the hell away from my father. Do you understand me? He's running for President. He can't afford to be mixed up in your stupid hijinks.

TISH. Hijinks with The Ronald! Yeah!

[AUGUSTINA *moves toward him flirtatiously and knees him in the groin.*]

TISH [*doubled-over*]. Ooof!

AUGUSTINA. Do we understand each other?

TISH. Stay away...from...The Ronald. Got it.

[*The elevator dings, the doors open. Enter* HARVEY, *stepping off the elevator.* TISH, *doubled-over, exits via the elevator. Enter* THE RONALD *from the wings, stepping onto the platform stage behind the lectern.* LIBBY *sits with her back to the audience, facing* THE RONALD.]

LIBBY. Governor, your state has been—

THE RONALD [*gesturing at his invisible debate opponents*]. Hey, Uncle Ben...is my rice done yet? And you, Senator Spicky, your plan on immigration...[*changes to a Spanish, Ricky Ricardo accent*]...you got some 'splainin' to do my friend!

LIBBY. Sir, the question was for the Governor of Florida.

[THE RONALD *comes out from behind the lectern.* AUGUSTINA *and* HARVEY *step onto either end of the platform stage swinging a jump rope.* THE RONALD *jumps rope as he talks.*]

THE RONALD. I'll take it for him, Libby. In fact, I'll answer for *all* of these nitwits.

[*He gestures expansively at the ten other invisible candidates on stage with him.*]

THE RONALD. Look at these guys. Have you ever seen such a collection of losers and wimps in your entire life? I just want to line them all up and kick them in the balls. I don't know why we're even *having* these debates. None of these pansies can beat the Liberals. Johnny Two-Percent down there on the end? Yeah, you. You're pathetic. You look like Beaker from *The Muppet Show. Mee-mee-mee-mee-mee-mee-mee!* And fat-ass down on the other end? Folks, I've been watching him the whole debate. He's had one eye on the craft services table, where…I want to say something to the people of Freedomland.

LIBBY. Sir, there's no time, and besides—

THE RONALD [*still jumping rope*]. It'll only take a second. Citizens of Freedomland! Hi, The Ronald here. I give you my solemn pledge. See all of these career politicians up here? All of these stupid, corrupt, dick-less, lying brain farts? If I become President, I vow this to the people of Freedomland: I'll round all of them up and throw them in Federal prison with Veronica McClintock. Then I'm going to institute term limits in the form of public beheadings of corrupt senators, and I'm going to hire ISIS to do the head-choppings. I vow this to you. Okay, Libby, back to you.

[*The* DINER PATRONS *stare at smartphones as they sip coffee.*]

DINER PATRON #1. God, I'm loving The Ronald more every day. Did you *hear* what he called them? I hate those scumbags. I wish we could exile 'em all to an island and drop a nuke on 'em.

DINER PATRON #2. Damn…how sweet would that be? Know what I love most about him? That he's not one of them. Total outsider. No political experience whatsoever.

DINER PATRON #1. Yeah, I know what you mean. He's white, he went to an Ivy League school, he's a Republitarian, and he's worth billions, but he's not *one* of them. He's fantastic.

DINER PATRON #2. I like how they're all scared shitless of the guy, looking at each other, waiting for somebody to *do* something. They want to yell or punch him, but they know they can't because that'd make 'em look un-presidential.

DINER PATRON #1. Meanwhile, The Ronald couldn't care less about looking presidential. Guy calls it like he sees it. I think he's the real deal.

DINER PATRON #2. Me too. That's why I gave a hundred bucks to his campaign. I'm six months behind in child support, but this election's too important, you know?

DINER PATRON #1. I do know.

[HARVEY *and* THE RONALD *are standing at the desk, flipping through the Cork Brothers' playbook, when the gold telephone rings.* HARVEY *answers it.*]

HARVEY. Hello? Yes. Who?

THE RONALD. Who is it?

HARVEY. Sir, it's the Democratic Dictator of the New and Improved USSR—Boris Buttinski.

THE RONALD. Boris! What a character! Lemme talk to him.

[THE RONALD *hustles to the telephone.*]

THE RONALD. Boris! How are you, comrade?…Uh-huh. Siberia? They're an endangered species, huh?…In the snow? Shirtless? And a hot tub afterwards with your personal harem?…Sure, count me in.…Yeah? Thanks. They *are* all losers, aren't they?…The election? Oh, you are? Uh-huh. Interesting.…Well, keep me in the loop. See you in January. Bye.

[THE RONALD *hangs up.*]

THE RONALD. Hmm. Know how we guarantee my safety, Harv?

HARVEY. No, sir. How?

THE RONALD. We give me a total douchebag for a running mate. Nobody'll want anything to happen to me because, if anything did, they'd get the douchebag, whoever that is.

HARVEY. I see what you mean, sir. Built-in insurance. So…where should we get him?

THE RONALD. I don't know. Just pick a guy…from the heartland. One of the flyovers. Somebody that'll play to values voters.

HARVEY. I'll get right on it, sir.

[HARVEY *goes to the elevator and punches the button.* THE RONALD *crosses to the swivel chair and sits down. The elevator dings, the doors open. Enter* AUGUSTINA, *unbuttoning her blouse as she walks in.* HARVEY *exits via the elevator.* AUGUSTINA *sits on her father's lap and leans back against him.* THE RONALD *peers down into her cleavage.*]

THE RONALD. Are we *sure* you're my biological daughter?

AUGUSTINA [*slapping his arm*]. Oh, Daddy…you always say that.

[THE RONALD *wraps his arms around her and types on a cell phone.*]

AUGUSTINA. Are you Facetwitting or Twitbooking again, Daddy?

THE RONALD. Uh-huh.

AUGUSTINA. What are you saying this time?

THE RONALD. Oh…nothing really. Just that all illegal immigrants kill babies with crucifixes.

AUGUSTINA. Daddy! You really have to start behaving more Presidential.

THE RONALD. You mean I have to be *politically correct.* No thanks, Princess.

AUGUSTINA. It's just that…lately…I get the feeling you actually *believe* these things you're saying.

[THE RONALD *starts bouncing* AUGUSTINA *on his lap,* and *she grinds against him.*]

THE RONALD. So…what does my favorite little girl want for Christmas this year?

AUGUSTINA. I dunno.

THE RONALD. Oh, there must be something.

AUGUSTINA. Well, there is one little thing, but…

THE RONALD. No buts, Princess.

AUGUSTINA. Forget it, it's impossible.

THE RONALD. Princess…with your father, all things are possible. Come now, tell me.

AUGUSTINA. Well, Daddy, I've been thinking. I know you hired that outside woman to be your campaign manager.

THE RONALD. Josie?

AUGUSTINA. Yeah, her. But I'm smarter than her, and I think I'd be a better campaign manager. Nobody knows The Ronald like I do. And haven't I been a good little girl running your empire the way I have? I've given you sixteen consecutive quarters of profitability and growth, and I've—

THE RONALD. You don't have to convince me, Princess. You've been wonderful. You're my spitting image. You got my gene for excellence—a gene that skipped over your knucklehead brothers.

AUGUSTINA. So why didn't you make *me* your campaign manager, Daddy?

THE RONALD. Because you're priceless to me, and this Josie chick is disposable.

AUGUSTINA. I don't understand.

THE RONALD. As the face of my campaign, Josie is going to get attacked and abused, and by the time I win, she's going to be a used-up Atlantic City hooker. Meanwhile, my little girl will still be fresh and beautiful, and none of the attacks on me will be associated with you.

AUGUSTINA. Then she's just the spokesperson for the campaign. She's not really running things. Right?

THE RONALD. Not at all. Do you think your Daddy would put a middle-aged neo-Nazi tart ahead of his own precious Princess?

AUGUSTINA. No…I guess not.

THE RONALD. You're going to be in the background, Augustina. That's always where the real power is anyway.

You're in my inner circle. You and Harv are my closest advisors.

AUGUSTINA. So, when you win, what will my job be?

THE RONALD. What job do you want?

AUGUSTINA. Chief of Staff.

THE RONALD. That's not a job you want, Princess. Trust me, you don't want all of that making the trains run on time crap. I was thinking of something better.

AUGUSTINA. Like what?

THE RONALD [*bouncing her in his lap*]. Well…how about First Lady? Sapphire's going to stay here when we win. You'd live in the executive mansion with me and be First Lady. And you'd be my special, secret advisor. You'd continue to run our empire for us, and you wouldn't have to be at my side twenty-four seven the way my Chief of Staff has to.

AUGUSTINA. But First Lady, Daddy? I'm married.

THE RONALD. You are? To who?

AUGUSTINA. I forget his name.

[*While* THE RONALD *continues to bounce* AUGUSTINA *on his lap, downstage* LIBBY *mugs to the audience.*]

LIBBY. Fellow Liberals, The Ronald's campaign has been burying the truth in an *avalanche* of lies! A mudslide of lies! A tsunami of lies! It's time for a fact-check.

Coming up…after the break. Smugedy-smug-smug, *lorem ipsum liberalum intelligentsium superioridum!*

[LIBBY *exits via the wings.*]

THE RONALD. Princess, there's another reason I want you to be First Lady. You see, there's a possibility they're going to make me put our empire in a blind trust. I don't even know what that means…"blind trust." The only people I trust are family, and top on that list is you, Princess.

AUGUSTINA. Really, Daddy? Oh…you're so wonderful to me.

[AUGUSTINA *kisses him on the cheek and wriggles against his lap as* THE RONALD *continues to bounce her.*]

THE RONALD. You don't mind if Daddy bounces his little girl, do you?

AUGUSTINA. Of course not, Daddy. I love it. So…who are "they"—the ones that'll make you put the empire in a blind trust?

THE RONALD. You know…those ethics people.

AUGUSTINA. Oh…*them.* Bunch of Kant worshipers.

THE RONALD. Princess! Don't say that word.

AUGUSTINA. No, Daddy, not the C-word. *Kant*, spelled K-A-N-T. Rhymes with "aunt." I studied him when I got my Ivy League education, at the same *Ivy League* school you went to. Kant was a philosopher, and a major tight-ass about ethics and lying. Did you know…he said you should *never* tell a lie, not even if you're hiding somebody from a killer and the killer shows up and asks if that person is in your house. If the killer asks, you have to tell him the truth and say, "Yeah, he's here. I'll get him for you while you sharpen up your axe."

THE RONALD. That makes no sense.

[*As* AUGUSTINA *prattles on about ethics,* THE RONALD *bounces her faster on his lap. She takes out a cell phone and types on it, while grinding and gyrating on top of him.*]

AUGUSTINA. It's pretty brilliant. He says the reason why you *always* have to tell the truth—even if a murderer is looking for someone and you know the murderer is going to kill that person—is that if you lie, you become responsible for everything that happens as a result of the lie. It's really complicated, but basically what it comes down to is…if you tell the murderer the truth, what the murderer does with that information is on him. The ball's back in his court. See, Daddy?

THE RONALD. Yes! [*Panting.*] I think…it's a stupid idea. "It is not the…truth that matters," Princess, "but… victory."

[THE RONALD *stops bouncing* AUGUSTINA.]

THE RONALD. By putting yourself in a situation where you always tell the truth, you lose all flexibility and leverage. If you want to be on the winning side, you can't be tied down to the truth all the time. If the truth is winning, go with the truth. If the lie wins, use the lie. This is how I'm going to win the election, Princess. You *do* know your Daddy is going to be the next President, right?

AUGUSTINA. I do, which is why I want a more powerful role. I want to be President someday, too. I want you to crush Veronica McClintock's dried-up ovaries in a vise, Daddy, so in eight years—or four, if you get bored with the job—*I* can be the first woman President.

THE RONALD. Hmm. All right, let's negotiate on this. I taught you how to negotiate. Do it. Get a better deal for yourself.

AUGUSTINA. Well, if I were going to negotiate the way you taught me to, I wouldn't say a damn thing. I'd sit here all day and say nothing. I'd make *you* make the first offer. Because—

THE RONALD. The side that offers terms first loses. Good girl.

AUGUSTINA. But we have more important things to do today, so I'm just going to tell you what I want. I want you to put that ultra-right-wing douchebag on the ticket. When you win, we let him be VP for a year or two—long enough to placate those freaks—and then we implicate him in a major scandal and you nominate *me* as your VP. The Senate, which will be Republitarian, will confirm me I'm sure, making me the heir apparent.

THE RONALD. I'd like to do that, Princess, but what about those anti-nepotism laws?

AUGUSTINA. Mm. Those laws make no sense to me. How else do people get jobs, if not because of who they know?

THE RONALD. Beats me. All right, we'll see what we can do. For now, though, I want you to be First Lady, run the empire and keep your brothers from being an embarrassment. You'll be my super-special, secret advisor and—

AUGUSTINA. Will I have walk-in privileges, Daddy?

THE RONALD. I don't know, Princess. There are probably going to be some top-secret situations that—

AUGUSTINA. Because if I didn't have walk-in privileges, Daddy, I wouldn't feel special. And if I didn't feel special, I wouldn't let you bounce me on your lap anymore.

THE RONALD. You wouldn't?

[AUGUSTINA *pouts and shakes her head.*]

THE RONALD. Okay, then. You'll always have walk-in privileges.

AUGUSTINA. No matter what?

THE RONALD. No matter what.

AUGUSTINA [*kissing him*]. Thank you, Daddy.

[*She gets up and smooths out her skirt.* THE RONALD *stands as well.*]

THE RONALD. I'm going to freshen up, Princess. What are you doing now?

AUGUSTINA. I'm meeting Reagan for lunch.

THE RONALD. Who? President Reagan?

AUGUSTINA. No, Daddy, President Reagan's dead. I'm talking about *Reagan*—your second daughter. Hello…?

THE RONALD. Oh, right. What's her net worth by the way?

AUGUSTINA. Between half a million and a million, I think.

THE RONALD. What a loser. You're worth what…a hundred and fifty million?

AUGUSTINA. About that.

THE RONALD. And you've got firmer breasts than her, *and* she's got those fat chipmunk cheeks, which make her like a seven. You're a nine, nine-and-a-half—

AUGUSTINA. Hmmph. I'm not a ten, Daddy?

THE RONALD. There's always room for improvement, Princess. Besides, the hotness scale is like the Richter scale for earthquakes. A nine-and-a-half is like seventy-five times hotter than a seven.

[*The elevator dings, the doors open.* HARVEY *enters.* THE RONALD *exits through one of the gold doors.*]

HARVEY [*to* AUGUSTINA]. Where's he going?

AUGUSTINA [*holds up two fingers while looking at her phone*]. I'm worried about my father, Harv. Has he seemed off to you at all?

HARVEY. Off, how?

AUGUSTINA. The social media outbursts for one thing.

HARVEY. Mmm, not really. What else?

AUGUSTINA. I'm worried he's developing Alzheimer's. He didn't remember who Reagan was.

HARVEY. The former President!

AUGUSTINA. No, you idiot—my younger sister, his *daughter*.

HARVEY. Oh.

AUGUSTINA. I've tried talking to him about being more Presidential, but he doesn't…

[*As she reads her smart phone, an expression of shock comes over her face.*]

HARVEY. Anything wrong?

AUGUSTINA. Oh. My. *GOD!* I have to go. Damage control. I'll be on LBN soon. Watch me.

[*She makes a call and holds the cell phone to her ear as she exits via the elevator.* THE RONALD *enters from behind the other gold door. A toilet flushes in the background.*]

THE RONALD. Where's August?

HARVEY. She just left. Said something about damage control, that we should watch her on LBN.

[THE RONALD *and* HARVEY *sit in the swivel chair and on the sofa, watching the action downstage.* LIBBY *runs breathlessly onstage from the wings, sits at the table and shuffles papers nervously.* AUGUSTINA *enters calmly from the opposite wings and sits at the table beside her. The "news theme" plays and fades out quickly.*]

LIBBY. Liberals, are you ready for this? Stick a fork in The Ronald's campaign for President, because he's *done.* What? You haven't heard? Well, wait for *it*.......! Ten-year-old video obtained by LBN shows The Ronald participating in a *fake blood drive* on college campuses, in which he and TV man-child Timmy Tish duped college coeds into giving blood topless! Here with me in the studio to a give an insultingly unapologetic, *pro forma* explanation of The Ronald's behavior is his daughter and corporate CEO Augustina. Augustina, thank you for joining us.

AUGUSTINA. Thank *you* for giving me a chance to clear up this misunderstanding.

LIBBY. That's what it is, a *misunderstanding?* To be clear, Augustina, the video *does* show your father in a Winnebago, watching Timmy Tish coerce college girls into taking off their shirts and bras and giving blood. The Ronald is in the background the entire time, sniggering.

AUGUSTINA. You see, Libby, that's the problem. My father doesn't snigger. The man doesn't laugh at all, in fact. Which is why I don't think that's him in the video. Besides, the man in that video has a medical mask on the whole time. You can't see his face.

LIBBY. But your father's uh, hairstyle, is very distinctive. It's clearly him.

AUGUSTINA. No, it was more likely one of his body doubles. You see, Libby, my father can't possibly be at every ribbon-cutting, which is why the corporation employs several actors to stand in for him. This is clearly one of those actors. I already have our corporate security investigating the matter.

LIBBY [*flustered, shuffling through papers*]. But…how can that be? Well, let's assume it was a body double in the video. That doesn't change the fact that your father has a *long* history of saying awful things about women. He's rated their body parts on social media. He has called into shock jock radio stations and referred to attractive female celebrities as, and I quote, "tit-sicles," "AI sex toys" and "schlong couplers." *"Schlong couplers,"* Augustina. And he's spoken of women he does *not* find attractive as, quote, "leather-faced lesbians" and "diesel dyke badger bitches."

AUGUSTINA [*smiling, shaking her head*]. He *has* said all of those things, the scamp. And it truly is reprehensible of him, Libby. I've spoken to him about behaving in a more presidential manner. All I can say is, the couple of times I screwed up on business deals, he called me much, much worse, believe me.

LIBBY. But that doesn't excuse him from—

AUGUSTINA. Libby, the thing you have to understand about my father is—and all of Freedomland needs to know this about him—he's what I call an equal opportunity insulter. Yes, he's said some terrible things about women, but men aren't exempt from his wrath either. I've heard him call my older brothers, quote, "brainless hermaphrodites" and "versions zero-point-one and zero-point-two." I've heard him call Jews, quote, "foreskin-obsessed matzo-eaters." He's referred to the Indians—our Native Freedomlanders—as, quote, "redskin alcoholic land squatters." And on the same day he said that, he insulted the Grand Xenophobe of the Xenophobic Xanthines of Xanadu—the notorious Hoodie Jones—calling him, quote, "a buck-toothed, inbred, pillowcase-wearing retard." So...you can see, Libby... [smiling] ...there's plenty of outrage to go around. But...on the positive side...I think there's something deeply refreshing about my father. Unlike all of the career politicians out there, he's not afraid to call things as he sees them. Instead of getting bogged down in politically correct rhetoric, The Ronald wants to bypass all of that nonsense and act on the issues that affect the people of Freedomland. Which is why he is going to win this election, Libby. Just wait and see.

LIBBY [smirking]. August...I admire your sociopathic unflappability cloaked in femininity.

AUGUSTINA. Thank you, Libby.

LIBBY. Well…like you said…we'll see.

[*The* DINER PATRONS *stare at smartphones as they sip coffee.*]

DINER PATRON #1. Boy, she sure told that Liberal bitch, huh? Now that's a *real* feminist—smoking hot, smart, and secure enough in her own womanhood to apologize for her father's so-called sexist comments.

DINER PATRON #2. That Augustina's exactly what a woman should be—polite, poised and well-spoken. Sugar and spice and everything nice.

DINER PATRON #1. Know what I wish?

DINER PATRON #2. What?

DINER PATRON #1. I wish I could bend her over this table and nail her while she reads Ann Coulter to me.

DINER PATRON #2 [*sighs*]. Yeah. Me too.

[AUGUSTINA *goes upstage and sits on the sofa beside* HARVEY.]

THE RONALD. Good job, Princess. Harv and I were watching the whole time. You spun that well.

AUGUSTINA. I wouldn't have had to, if *Harv* had gotten rid of Timmy a long time ago. Where is Timmy, by the way?

[*The elevator dings, the doors open.*]

THE RONALD. Ah. Timmy?

[TISH *takes one step out of the elevator.*]

TISH. Yeah?

THE RONALD. You're fired.

[TISH *spins on his heels and exits back into the elevator.*]

THE RONALD. And I've already hired your replacement.

[*The* DELIVERYBOY *enters from the elevator, and the doors close.*]

DELIVERYBOY. Large plain cheese?

THE RONALD. Put it on the desk, along with your ready cash. And throw in your belt.

[THE RONALD *swaggers over to the platform stage.* LIBBY, *at her table, faces him. The "news theme" plays and fades out quickly. She turns to the audience.*]

LIBBY. Good evening, Freedomland, and welcome to the first and only Presidential debate. We already know Veronica McClintock is going to be our next President, but out of politeness to The Ronald, and so our network's insipid Saturday night sketch comedy show can get some desperately needed material, we are proud to bring you this debate. The first question is to The Ronald.

THE RONALD. Hi, Libby. Hi, Freedomland. Great to be here.

Libby. Sir, my first question is—

The Ronald. To be perfectly honest with you, right now I'd prefer to be at one of my hundreds of luxury properties around the world, probably playing a round of golf on one of my fine courses—some of the best courses in the universe. Fairways so green, you'll think you're playing on a giant dollar bill, I guarantee you. In fact, to all Republitarians and Undecideds out there, I extend this offer. When you go into the voting booth next week, take a photo of your ballot where you vote for me, email it to my campaign website, and you'll receive a coupon for a free non-alcoholic beverage, to be given to you in your vehicle at the gate of any of my fine properties! Just a little incentive for—

Libby. Sir, are you publicly bribing voters to vote for you?

The Ronald [*shrugs*]. It's not a bribe, Libby. It's an incentive program. You wouldn't understand because you're not a business genius like me. What's your question?

Libby. Sir, you've been very vocal about your policy on illegal immigration, but—

The Ronald [*checking his watch, motioning "speed it up"*]. Let's go, Libby. Gotta go, gotta go!

Libby. *But*, so far in this entire campaign you haven't said a word about what you want to *do* as President. What is The Ronald's vision for Freedomland?

The Ronald. Okay, I'll keep my answer simple, Libby, so you and all the Liberal welfare-worshippers out there can understand it. Here it is. I'm going to get better deals for Freedomland. Better deals from everybody, across the board. I'm the best negotiator in the universe, I know how to negotiate. I'm going to get the moat. I'm going to get the cyber. I'm going to get the pre-existing. I'm going—

LIBBY. The pre-existing *what*, sir?

THE RONALD. Let me finish. I'm going to get the weapons. I'm going to get the jobs. I'm going to get the rights. I'm going to get the roads. I'm going to get the tax cuts. I'm going to get the terrorists. I'm going to get the trade deals. If there's anything to get, The Ronald is going to get it—for Freedomland. Vote for me, and I'll make Freedomland *fantastic* again. I guarantee you.

[THE RONALD *walks off the stage and sits in his chair.* AUGUSTINA *sits at the desk upstage and leafs through the giant playbook. The* DELIVERYBOY *sits on the sofa beside* HARVEY *eating pizza. The elevator dings, the doors open. Enter the* PROFESSOR, BAILEY, FORBES *and* TREASURY. *The two sons wear suits and throw a football around.*]

FORBES. Election night, Pop! We're all here to watch you win.

TREASURY. What kind of pizza is that, dude?

DELIVERYBOY. Large plain cheese?

FORBES [*to* TREASURY]. Hey, go long!

[FORBES *throws a pass way off course, which is caught by one of the* DINER PATRONS. *The other patron looks at his smartphone.*]

DINER PATRON #1. Returns are coming in. Country's going redder than The Ronald's tie, I'm telling you.

DINER PATRON #2. If he gets Pennsylvania, McClintock's toast.

[*Downstage,* LIBBY *is slumped over her table.*]

LIBBY. Fellow flaming Liberals of Freedomland, I have failed you. I have more than failed you—I caused this calamity. In our smugness, I and my colleagues in the media underestimated The Ronald. We reported and commented on his antics because he boosted our ratings…when what we should have done from the very beginning was ignore him. If we'd ignored him, he would have gone to the scrapheap of political might-have-beens. Indeed, we failed you. But our Liberal candidate Veronica McClintock failed us all—in her arrogance of campaigning not to us voters and the issues affecting our families, but to the electoral map. As for my own shame, I cannot live with it. And so I must follow in the footsteps of my idol, Socrates, the father of rational thought…by drinking hemlock.

[*She reaches under the table, pulls out a chalice, walks around the table and sits on top of it, facing the audience. Raising the chalice in one hand, she holds up the forefinger of her other hand as she speaks. This pose mimics Socrates' in Jacques Louis-David's painting* The Death of Socrates.]

LIBBY. Well, now it is time to be off, I to die and you to live in a country under The Ronald. But which of us has the happier prospect is unknown to anyone but God. [*She gulps down the contents of the chalice.*] Ugh, like a bad Merlot. [*She convulses, chokes, lies back on the desk.*] O, I die, sweet Freedomland. The potent poison quite o'er-crows my spirit. I cannot live to hear the news from network; but I do prophesy the election lights on The Ronald. [*Takes her last breath.*] The rest is…silence. [*She dies.*]

[*The* DINER PATRONS *are staring at smartphones as they sip coffee.*]

DINER PATRON #1. Jeezum Crow, did you see that? Woman killed herself right on TV.

DINER PATRON #2. Don't see that every day, that's for sure.

DINER PATRON #1. That's for sure.

DINER PATRON #2. Good riddance. One less smart-mouthed Liberal in the world.

DINER PATRON #1. You can say that again. I wonder if The Ronald was watching.

[*Timmy* TISH *runs on stage from the wings, snatches the glasses off* LIBBY'S *face, puts them on, and runs offstage opposite, leaving her dead body on top of the table. Upstage, the gold telephone rings.* AUGUSTINA *answers it.*]

AUGUSTINA [*speaking into the phone*]. Hello? Yes, he's here, Madam Governor. Hang on. [*Calls loudly to* THE RONALD, *but doesn't cover the phone mouthpiece.*] Daddy? It's that dried-up Liberal whore calling to surrender! I mean concede. [*Speaking sweetly into phone again.*] He's coming, Madam Governor.

[THE RONALD *walks over to the phone, doing a little victory dance by shaking a box of breath mints and dumping them into his mouth and over his face onto the floor.*]

THE RONALD [*to* AUGUSTINA]. We did it, Princess. Or should I say, "First Lady"?

[THE RONALD *shakes the rest of the mints onto* AUGUSTINA, *who rubs her body and pretends she's showering in them. She kisses him on the lips and hands him the receiver.*]

THE RONALD [*speaking into the phone*]. Hi, Veronica, what's up?…Oh? Fantastic. You're a tough competitor, Veronica. Listen…all that stuff about throwing you in Federal prison? Forget it. That was just crap I had to say. Yeah, the right-wing wackjobs wanted to see you in an orange jumpsuit.…I know, I know. Don't worry about it. I'm going downstairs now and I'll say a bunch of nice stuff about you.…No, I don't want any of those Control-Alt-Delete morons trying to take you out either. So what do you think you'll do now…now that you're retired?…Uh-huh. Yeah?… Well, good luck. Goodnight.

[THE RONALD *hangs up the telephone and walks in a daze to the mirror, where he gives himself a double thumbs-up.*]

Augustina. Well, Daddy?

The Ronald. She conceded. You're looking at the next President of Freedomland. As soon as that shambling, goofy-eared, boring black guy leaves office, that is.

[*Everyone claps and cheers.* The Ronald *looks around nodding and raises his hands to silence them.*]

The Ronald. Where's Sapphire? I thought I was married.

Augustina. You are married. She's meeting us down in the ballroom.

The Ronald. Is that what you're wearing?

Augustina. You don't like it, Daddy?

The Ronald. I don't like it. Put on your ballet tutu. I want the whole world to see those gorgeous gams of yours, not to mention your awesome rack. Remember—the hotter you look, Princess, the better I look. [*Pointing at his groin with both hands.*] I want everybody knowing you sprang from *my* incredible loins, got it?

Augustina. Of course, Daddy. I'll change before we go on stage.

The Ronald. And where's six-year-old mini-me?

Augustina [*confused*]. Oh…*Viscount.* I think he's sleeping, Daddy.

THE RONALD. Well, somebody wake his skinny ass up. I want him standing right beside me during my speech. Think of how vigorous I'll look, the incredible *sta-min-ah* I'll show—a distinguished older gentleman wide awake while a six-year-old punk is falling asleep next to him!

AUGUSTINA. A brilliant idea, Daddy. I'll have Sapphire wake him up and dress him and brush his teeth and tie his shoes and comb his hair to look exactly like yours.

THE RONALD. Excellent. All right. Let's do this thing.

[*Exeunt everyone into the elevator.*]

CURTAIN

Act III

SCENE— *The high-rise penthouse lair, with a couple of set changes. The small platform stage is now empty. Downstage, the LBN news table is still in place, but on the other side, the diner booth has been replaced by the putting green. Upstage, AUGUSTINA sits on the edge of the desk. She is talking on the gold telephone and looking at a smartphone in her other hand.*

AUGUSTINA. No, don't put me back on hold. I've been holding for half an hour. Do I really need to remind you who I am? This is Augustina, daughter of The Ronald, the President-Elect of Freedomland. I'm CEO of The Ronald Corporation, so I handle all problems like this one. No, no—I…I don't care what your policy is.

[*The elevator dings, the doors open. Enter* HARVEY. *He sees* AUGUSTINA *on the phone and walks over.*]

AUGUSTINA [*into phone*]. You're useless. I want to speak to a manager. No. No. Get me a manager. Get me a manager. Get me a manager. Get me a manager. Good.

HARVEY. What's going on?

AUGUSTINA [*to* HARVEY]. Oh, just another little mess. The kind of mess I've become incredibly good at cleaning up for my father. Somebody at Joogolplex got cute and— [*Speaking into phone.*] Yes, I'm here. What is your name again? Randal? Okay. And did the representative explain the situation, or do…? Of course she didn't. Well, Randal, this is very simple. I'm the CEO of The Ronald Corporation and daughter of the President-Elect. I'm looking at the Joogolplex map listing for our headquarters, okay? The name of this building—the building I'm in right now—is, quote, "The Ronald Sky Palace." Do you follow me so far? Good. Here's the problem, Randal. Either somebody hacked your system, or you have a politically disgruntled employee, because the name has been changed. Changed to what? It's now, quote, "Clown Shithouse."

[Harvey *remains stoic.*]

Augustina [*into phone*]. Yes. Now, Randal...my father—the President-Elect—he doesn't know about this yet. Therefore, I strongly suggest you get this fixed immediately, before he does find out. Otherwise, who knows...the CEOs of Joogolplex might find themselves suddenly without Freedomland citizenship. My father harbors grudges, Randal. Yes, yes, exactly. Good. Then I'll expect it fixed in the next five minutes. Goodbye.

[*She hangs up.*]

Harvey. You wanted to see me?

Augustina. What the hell is wrong with my father, Harv? You've worked for him for...what?

Harvey. Forty years.

Augustina. Forty years. So maybe you can tell me...is he crazy?

HARVEY. What gives you that idea?

AUGUSTINA. Harv, he hasn't been right since he announced his candidacy. That was almost two years ago. I thought the crazy talk would stop when he won, but it's just gotten worse. Yesterday, he—

[*The elevator dings, the doors open. Enter* THE RONALD *and the* DELIVERYBOY. THE RONALD *wears the pizza delivery hat, jacket, jeans and sneakers, and the* DELIVERYBOY *wears a navy suit and red tie.* AUGUSTINA *ducks behind the desk and pulls* HARVEY *down with her.*]

AUGUSTINA. Stay down. Watch.

HARVEY. Why is he dressed like that?

AUGUSTINA. See what I mean? I have no idea. I think he's gone insane, Harv.

HARVEY. But…?

AUGUSTINA. But *what*? Look at him. The press can't see him like this.

DELIVERYBOY. T.R., I have to use the bathroom.

THE RONALD. Number one or number two?

DELIVERYBOY. Two. Pretty sure.

THE RONALD. Then you'd say, "I've gotta go drop a deuce." Say it.

DELIVERYBOY. I've gotta go drop a deuce.

THE RONALD [*correcting his pronunciation*]. Deuce.

DELIVERYBOY. Deuce.

THE RONALD. All right, it's through those doors.

DELIVERYBOY. Which one?

THE RONALD. I don't know. One of them.

[*The* DELIVERYBOY *exits through one of the gold doors.* THE RONALD *walks over to the putting green. He picks up the putter and looks at it with a vacant expression on his face.*]

HARVEY. Maybe he's just pretending. You know how your father likes playing tricks on people. Like the time he faked his death so he could see who showed up to the funeral.

AUGUSTINA. But I've never seen him this bad. Look at the poor wretch.

[THE RONALD *paces in circles around the putting green, studying the putter.*]

THE RONALD. What are you…a very long hammer?

[*He holds it by the club end, rests the grip on the floor and walks around.*]

THE RONALD. No…a cane. [*Pacing in circles.*] What am I going to do? Wanted to win, wanted to win, wanted to win, and I won. I won. I'm the next President. [*Panicked.*] I'm the next President! How could this happen? You knew you would win, but all you saw was the win, not the dreadful routine of *governing*. Ugh, it even *sounds* awful. *Governing*. Have to find a way out. Have to find a way out. But you can't quit, can't say you don't want to do it...because The Ronald *doesn't* quit. If The Ronald quits, it'll kill the value of his brand. The Ronald brand means luxury, means winning. No, have to find another way. All right...what if I didn't actually win? What if I called for a recount? No, *I* can't call for one, but Veronica McClintock—Mih-Clin-Tock—could. Recount. Recount. Recount!

[*As he rushes over to the gold telephone,* AUGUSTINA *and* HARVEY *crouch beneath the desk.* THE RONALD *picks up the phone and dials a number.*]

THE RONALD [*affecting a woman with a patrician accent*]. Yes, hello? Election fraud people? This is Veronica Mih-Clin-Tock...yes, the Presidential candidate. Yes it is. Is so. I am too a Liberal. Oh yeah? Here's the password. *Lorem ipsum liberalum intelligentsium superioridum.* Good. Now listen closely, young man. I am formally requesting a recount. Which states? Oh... anywhere it was close. Yes. Yes. That's good. There too. Seventeen million? Fine. You can bill my opponent, The Ronald. One question. How long are we talking? Uh-huh. Well, please get started. The people of Free-domland deserve a fair and honest democratic election outcome and all that Liberal...stuff. Goodbye. [*Hangs up, resumes his normal voice.*] It's worth a try.

[AUGUSTINA *gestures at* HARVEY, *and while* THE RONALD*'s back is turned, the two of them open one of the gold* *doors, slip inside and peek out the crack.* THE RONALD *turns to the window and gazes outside.*]

THE RONALD. Well, well, there you are, supermoon—the biggest supermoon until 2034. So...unless I take that vampire deal the Cork Brothers offered me, I'll never see you again. Frankly, I don't see what's so "super" about you. It's not like you're *that* much bigger. [*Snorts contemptuously.*] If you worked for me, supermoon... you know what you'd be? That's right...you'd be fired. Hear that, supermoon? You're fired. You're fired, supermoon. What've you ever done for *me*? Hmmph. You suck, supermoon.

[*Enter the* DELIVERYBOY *through the French doors, from the balcony.*]

THE RONALD. What are you doing out there?

DELIVERYBOY. Sorry, I get turned around in this place.

THE RONALD. I'm bored. Let's go deliver pizzas. And by "deliver pizzas," I mean—

DELIVERYBOY. Throw 'em off the Empire State Building. I feel you, bro.

THE RONALD. Don't feel me. I'm very, very, very heterosexual.

DELIVERYBOY. No, dude...I mean, like, I agree.

THE RONALD. Oh. Then just say that. No more colored talk, alright?

DELIVERYBOY. Sure.

[THE RONALD *and* DELIVERYBOY *bump fists and "blow it up," then exit via the elevator. The doors close.* AUGUSTINA *and* HARVEY *come out of hiding.*]

AUGUSTINA. See? Insane, I guarantee you.

HARVEY. Why do you and your father say that?

AUGUSTINA. Say what?

HARVEY. I guarantee you. You're offering people a guarantee.

AUGUSTINA. Shut up, Harv. We were talking about my father's mental state. He requested a recount. A *recount*, Harv. You heard him babbling. The man doesn't want to be President now. He must be insane.

HARVEY. So, let's bring it up to him. If he really doesn't want to be President now, there must be some way we can get him out of it.

AUGUSTINA. Oh, well…it doesn't matter anyway.

HARVEY. What do you mean?

AUGUSTINA. I *mean*…that once he's President, I can control things. There's precedent for it. After President Wilson had a stroke, his wife ran the country for like three years. If Daddy goes crazy while in office, I'll take care of him and act in his stead. After a year, I'll make him get rid of that right-wing douchebag Dick Dunce, and have him make *me* his VP. Then I'll have him declared mentally incompetent, and *I'll* become the first woman President.

HARVEY. Augustina, there's something you don't know.

AUGUSTINA. Oh? What's that, *Harv?*

HARVEY. Back about two years ago, when he decided he was going to run for President, he told me he was going to be saying and doing a lot of weird things.

AUGUSTINA. So?

HARVEY. So, he said I should never worry—even if it seems like he's gone completely batshit, he's just pretending.

AUGUSTINA. Why the hell would he do that, Harv?

HARVEY. Something about testing people's judgment and loyalties. Stuff like that.

AUGUSTINA. Well, maybe he started out *pretending*, but he's gone over the edge. Clearly. For example, *The Ronald* does not throw pizzas off high-rises.

HARVEY. Uh…

AUGUSTINA. What?

HARVEY. Nothing. So how do you want to handle this? What do we do?

AUGUSTINA. Nothing. We do nothing. Let's see how the rest of transition goes.

[*As* AUGUSTINA *and* HARVEY *exit via the elevator, down-stage* TISH *enters from the wings. He is wearing the black horn-rimmed glasses and sits in the reporter chair at the LBN table. The "news theme" plays and fades out quickly. He is stiff and talks to the camera (audience) awkwardly, as if he's having trouble reading from a teleprompter.*]

TISH. Hi. Welcome to the Timmy Tish Republitarian Variety show. I'm your host, Timmy Tish. It has been a bizarre ten weeks since the election, and President-Elect The Ronald has Republitarians all across Freedomland deeply uncertain. Time for the Republitarian recap. Smile. Pause. Straighten glasses. Just days after the election, Vice President-Elect Dick Dunce was assaulted with a cup of urine thrown in his face by an amusement park mascot. Later in November, Liberal Veronica McClintock called for a recount in seven states. Later it was revealed that President-Elect The Ronald had requested the recount. In December, The Ronald's bizarre behavior got even worse, when he was spotted dressed as a deliveryboy, delivering pizzas to the Electoral College, handing cash to the electors and screaming, "Vote for Veronica" and "I love welfare!" Luckily the Electoral College ignored him and fulfilled their Constitutional duty by voting for The Ronald, thus cementing him as our new President. He has made several questionable cabinet appointments. Including a woman billionaire with an IQ of 83 to run the Department of Education, and Hoodie Jones, leader of the X.X.X., as a new justice on the Supreme Court. Jones has sworn always to wear his hood during oral arguments and while delivering opinions, which has some lefty groups slightly uncomfortable. To which I say, Liberals…grow a pair. Pause. Adjust glasses. Straighten papers. Serious face. It's now only two days until inauguration, and this Republitarian is worried. Not only is The Ronald still dressed as a pizza deliveryboy, he has been donating to homeless shelters and orphanages, and he signed a petition demanding a national minimum wage of twenty-five dollars per hour. Naturally this has upset the Republitarian business establishment, which has a God-given right to make a million-percent profit on the backs of infinite cheap labor while enjoying the legal protections and political stability of Freedomland. Fellow Republitarians…quite simply…this is not The Ronald I have known and loved and fantasized about for twenty years. This is not The Ronald I voted for. Serious face. Sigh. Smile. Coming up on the Republitarian Variety Show, after the break. The always funny and homophobic Reverend Brimstone will share his break-dancing skills, and the new Speaker of the House sings "Fly Me to the Moon." Don't go away!

[Tish *exits via the wings. Upstage, the* Deliveryboy, *still wearing a suit and tie, enters from one of the gold doors and sits in the swivel chair. His back is to the elevator. The elevator dings, the doors open. Enter the Cork Brothers,* Chucky *and* Davey, *wearing their matching trenchcoats and fedoras.*]

Chucky. Hold it, Davey. Wait. There he is. The Ronald.

Davey. Back in his signature suit, I see.

Chucky. Yup. All alone and no idea we're here. Time to make him one of us.

Davey. Good idea. I'll do it. I could use a little pick-me-up anyway.

[Davey *sneaks up behind the* Deliveryboy *and bites his neck. The* Deliveryboy *screams and faints in the chair.*]

Chucky. Good. When he comes around, he'll be one of us.

[*Enter* The Ronald *through one of the gold doors. He's wearing the pizza delivery outfit and looking at a smartphone.*]

The Ronald. Hey, pizzaboy, we got two million more online signatures on the minimum wage thing. What are you screaming about, anyway?

Chucky. Oh, crap. Davey...*that's* The Ronald.

Davey. What? Who'd I bite then?

[*The* Deliveryboy *springs up in the chair. His eyes pop open like he's in a trance.*]

Deliveryboy. Large plain cheese?

The Ronald. Dammit. What did you guys do?

Deliveryboy. Large plain cheese?

The Ronald. He was my body double, guys. I needed him.

DELIVERYBOY. Large plain cheese?

THE RONALD. Don't go to a doctor, pizzaboy. They're useless. Let it heal. Let it heal.

DAVEY. Come with me, son.

[DAVEY *helps the* DELIVERYBOY *out of the chair, walks him out to the balcony and pushes him off the building.* DAVEY *walks back in dusting his hands and closes the French doors.*]

DAVEY. Sorry, honest mistake.

CHUCKY. Happens. We *have* been doing this for a *thousand* years, Davey.

DAVEY. Yeah.

THE RONALD. You guys thought he was me, didn't you?

DAVEY. No, of course not.

CHUCKY. But we do have a bone to pick with you, mister. We gave you—

DAVEY. One-point-one billion dollars to win this election. You're not even President yet, and—

CHUCKY. You're already doing one of the things we told you *not* to do, which is to bring up the issue of—

DAVEY. Income inequality. Idiot.

THE RONALD. I read my first book the other day, guys. *The Gospel of Wealth* by Andrew Carnegie. You know, the rich steel guy? He says that once you've made your money, you're obligated by God to give it all away.

CHUCKY [*flustered*]. Obligated…by God?! Who are you? [*To* DAVEY.] I told you he wasn't a T.R. we could work with.

DAVEY. Yeah, yeah. Save it.

CHUCKY [*turning to* THE RONALD *with bloodlust*]. But there's still time to—

DAVEY. Fix him. Good idea. I'll go this way, you go over there.

THE RONALD. You freaks better stay away from me! I'm warning you!

[DAVEY *and* CHUCKY *chase* THE RONALD *around the stage, through the gold doors, and in and out of the French doors. It's crazy farce time, where things happen like one of them exits via the elevator and enters a second later from the balcony. During the chase, during a moment when the stage is empty, the* ACTRESS, *the doppelgänger of Augustina, and dressed exactly like her (right down to her unbuttoned white blouse), enters via the elevator. She sits on the sofa flipping through a fashion magazine, with her back to the gold doors and the elevator.* DAVEY *and* CHUCKY *enter simultaneously from the two gold doors and stare at each other.*]

DAVEY. You get him?

CHUCKY. No, you?

DAVEY. Seriously? If I got him, why would I ask if *you* got him? Dumbass.

CHUCKY. I'm not the dumbass, you're the dumbass.

ACTRESS. Is that you, Daddy? Guess whose little girl is wearing black lingerie? I'm ready for my spanking.

DAVEY [*pointing at the sofa*]. Wait a second…that's Augustina, the daughter.

CHUCKY. Yeah, so?

DAVEY. So…we don't need The Ronald. *She's* the one we should have bought from the beginning. Turns out, she's ten times more Machiavellian than her father.

CHUCKY. Plus, she's hot with a stupendous rack, which means male voters won't notice that she's evil incarnate! I'll get her.

[*As* CHUCKY *sneaks up behind the* ACTRESS *and bites her neck,* THE RONALD *enters from the balcony. He's in his suit and tie and is holding something behind his back. The* ACTRESS *screams and faints on the sofa.*]

THE RONALD. What the hell!?

CHUCKY. Sorry, T.R., but we've got to protect our investment. Your daughter's been plotting against you anyway. Harvey Green called and told us about her plans.

DAVEY. She was going to have you make her VP, then get you declared mentally incompetent so she could assume the Presidency. She had to go.

THE RONALD. You idiots! That wasn't Augustina. That was a Broadway actress pretending to *be* Augustina. She was my Augustina lookalike schlong coupler! Morons!

[CHUCKY *and* DAVEY *look at each other, nod and start toward* THE RONALD, *who produces a crucifix from behind his back and holds it in front of them. The Cork Brothers recoil from it and hiss. The* ACTRESS *springs up in the chair. Her eyes pop open like she's in a trance.*]

ACTRESS. Five-six-seven-eight! Step-ball-change-kick-turn-kick-turn-and—

THE RONALD. Take her with you. Stupid jerks. Ruined a perfectly good schlong coupler. Looked *just like* Augustina.

ACTRESS. Five-six-seven-eight! Step-ball-change-kick-turn-kick-turn-and—

DAVEY. Come with us, honey.

[DAVEY *and* CHUCKY *help the* ACTRESS *up and walk with her to the elevator. The elevator doors open. Inside the compartment is the* DELIVERYBOY, *covered in blood.*]

DELIVERYBOY. Large plain cheese?

CHUCKY. The Ronald hasn't heard the last of us. We want our money back. And give me our book.

THE RONALD. No. I'm not finished with it yet. And I already spent the money, so there.

CHUCKY. I knew it! I knew you were a debtor!

DAVEY. Come on, Chucky!

[*Exeunt* DAVEY, CHUCKY *and the* ACTRESS *into the elevator. The elevator doors close.* THE RONALD *walks to the swivel chair and sits down. Enter the* SHOESHINE MAN *from one of the gold doors with his shoeshine kit. He begins to shine* THE RONALD*'s shoes.* THE RONALD *lets out a loud sigh.*]

SHOESHINE MAN. Sir, I was glad to see you turned your back on the Cork Brothers. All they're interested in is creating discontent. Discontented people spend money. They spend money so they can feel better. The Ronald has a big opportunity here. You could turn your back on the Republitarians and truly make Freedomland fantastic again. Do things they don't expect—like pushing for a livable national minimum wage. Bring industry back to Freedomland. And stay out of women's bodies and people's bedrooms. Focus on what The Ronald knows best—business. And if you do the kind of job that my boss thinks you might be capable of, you'll be remembered forever.

THE RONALD. Interesting. Sit on the sofa there. Where have I seen you before? What's your name?

[*The* SHOESHINE MAN *closes up his shine case and sits down on the sofa.*]

SHOESHINE MAN. Thank you, sir. It's Gabriel.

THE RONALD. Who's your boss? Is he Liberal or Republitarian?

SHOESHINE MAN. My boss is apolitical. My boss is neither male nor female. My boss is one and all, indivisible. My boss is everywhere, always, binding us, unifying us and—

THE RONALD. Like the Force.

SHOESHINE MAN. Sort of. My boss knows The Ronald's deepest desires. The secret petitions of your heart. The things you haven't told a living soul.

THE RONALD. Oh yeah? Name one.

SHOESHINE MAN. Like the fact that you want a colossal phallic monument to you in the capital.

THE RONALD. How did you...?

SHOESHINE MAN. Or how you want your picture to appear on a million-dollar bill. Or how, deep-down, you're really terribly insecure and you just want the world to love you. My boss has sent me to tell you...if you put service and kindness to others ahead of your own desires, you will receive all of those things and much, much more.

THE RONALD. It's tempting, but...I went to church a lot as a kid, and I've always remembered that line, "It is easier for a camel to pass through the eye of a needle than it is for a rich man to get into heaven."

SHOESHINE MAN. Yes, it's difficult for rich people to get in, but not impossible. Listen, you don't have to give us your answer today. After inauguration, I'll drop by and—

THE RONALD. No, that's okay. I've made my decision.

SHOESHINE MAN. You have? Well…could you tell me what it is? I have to go back to my boss and report.

THE RONALD. You'll see.

SHOESHINE MAN. Maybe I could leave some literature with you?

THE RONALD. I don't want any literature.

SHOESHINE MAN. Okay, then. Good luck.

THE RONALD. Thanks. Tell your boss I said hello.

[*The* SHOESHINE MAN *picks up his shine case and exits via the elevator.* THE RONALD *walks to the desk and makes a call on the gold telephone.*]

THE RONALD [*into phone*]. Get everyone up here. You too. It's time for a bunch of people to get fired.

[*He returns to the swivel chair.*]

THE RONALD. My favorite part.

[*The elevator dings, the doors open. Enter* AUGUSTINA, HARVEY, BAILEY, FORBES, TREASURY, *and the* PROFESSOR. THE RONALD *faces them, frowning. Bass-heavy, tension-filled music plays low in the background.*]

THE RONALD. Everybody over here. Stand in front of me. Good. It's been two years since I gave you all your marching orders. I told you…only one of you would be coming with me to the capital and getting a job with a *yooooge* salary…and the rest of you…would be fired. Professor, who do you think I should take with me? No, don't answer that. The fact is, you're all a bunch of deplorables and I already know who's been naughty and who's been nice and who should be fired. Augustina?

AUGUSTINA. Yes, Daddy?

THE RONALD. You're…

AUGUSTINA. I'm what, Daddy?

THE RONALD. Forbes? Treasury? Professor? Bailey? [*Pointing, rapid-fire, at each of them.*] You're fired. You're fired. You're fired. You're fired. Hit the bricks.

[*Exit* FORBES, TREASURY, BAILEY *and the* PROFESSOR *via the elevator.*]

THE RONALD. Now it's down to you two. And I've got to admit, it's a tough choice for me. Both of you betrayed me. But one worse than the other. Augustina?

AUGUSTINA. Yes, Daddy?

THE RONALD. I heard you were planning to have me declared mentally incompetent so you could take over the Presidency. Is this true?

AUGUSTINA. It is, Daddy. But it's what you would have done if you were me.

THE RONALD. Probably.

AUGUSTINA. Who told you? Harv?

THE RONALD. No. Harv…is it true you were making a deal for yourself with the Cork Brothers?

HARVEY. Not exactly, T.R.

THE RONALD. Harv, I think you're a terrific asset. Augustina?

AUGUSTINA [*tearfully*]. Am I fired, Daddy?

THE RONALD. Harv…you're fired. Get lost.

[*Exit* HARVEY *via the elevator.*]

THE RONALD. Okay, Princess, come sit on Daddy's lap.

[AUGUSTINA *sits on his lap.*]

AUGUSTINA. I have to admit, Daddy…you had me going there for a second. I thought I was getting fired.

THE RONALD. No you didn't.

AUGUSTINA. No, I didn't. I knew they were all a bunch of losers and that I'd win. I'm going to be a fantastic First Lady, Daddy, and in a year or so…I'll be a great Vice President.

THE RONALD. And tell you what…I'm only going to serve one term so then you can take over.

AUGUSTINA. Thanks, Daddy.

THE RONALD [*leering into her cleavage*]. I really don't think you're my biological daughter.

[*She smiles and kisses him. There is the sound of a helicopter outside.*]

AUGUSTINA. I called for Marine One an hour ago.

[THE RONALD *and* AUGUSTINA *walk to the French doors. He picks up the giant playbook.*]

THE RONALD. All right, Princess…let's do this thing.

[*As they walk outside,* THE RONALD *tosses the playbook off the balcony. The two of them round the corner out of sight. The helicopter noise loudens briefly, then fades into the distance.*]

THE END

THE CLEAN-SHAVEN SECRETARY
WITH THE PISTOL

CHARACTERS

CARTWRIGHT: A very clean-shaven man in his 20s; cheeks should gleam; wears a suit with a visible watch-chain that holds a pocket-watch.

MISS SULLIVAN: A young woman in her early to mid-20s; wears a period dress (late Victorian or early Edwardian), gloves and wide-brimmed hat with feathers.

B.A. NOYING: A middle-aged man; wears period clothing and a large sandwich board.

MR. DRAKE: The business owner, in his 50s or 60s; wears an old-fashioned suit or frock-coat with waistcoat.

MODEL: A young woman in her 20s or early 30s; wears a sexy TV game show hostess dress.

The PLAYWRIGHT: A handsome, witty man (Chris Orcutt, if available); wears a modern, dashing suit.

SETTING

The outer office and waiting room of a businessman, lawyer, accountant, architect, etc.; the exact business doesn't matter and shouldn't be specified.

TIME

Late 19th or early 20th century.

THE SCENE

An office waiting room. Against the upstage wall are a sofa and a desk. Both face downstage.

The office secretary, Cartwright, *is clean-shaven, but whether or not he possesses a pistol remains to be seen. As the scene opens, he hums or whistles to himself. He straightens papers on the desk, consults a pocket watch and nods crisply. He crosses to the outer office door, and consults his watch again with his free hand poised on the door lock.*

NOTE: *At the start of the play—until* B.A. Noying *enters—the actors perform the scene in a self-conscious, "presentational" style.*

Cartwright. And…now!

[*He snaps his watch shut and opens the door. Enter* Miss Sullivan. *A look of panic comes over* Cartwright.]

Cartwright. What are you doing here?

[Miss Sullivan *carries a little dog. Actually it is a stuffed prop of a little dog, a distinction that becomes important in a few minutes. She breezes past* Cartwright *and stands near his desk.*]

Miss Sullivan. I demand to see Mr. Drake this instant!

Cartwright [*nervous*]. I am afraid that is impossible, Miss Sullivan, as Mr. Drake is otherwise engaged for the entire morning.

MISS SULLIVAN [*sitting*]. Then I shall wait here. I shall wait all day if necessary. I will be heard, Mr. Cartwright.

CARTWRIGHT. That is also impossible. Mr. Drake takes luncheon at one o'clock, and various meetings and appointments will occupy his time for the entire afternoon. [*He crosses to her, takes her gloved hand.*] Now, madam, may I suggest you go home? I will give you cab fare, if you like.

MISS SULLIVAN [*yanking her hand away*]. Cab fare? Cab fare! I will not be silenced for such a paltry sum. [*Loudly, towards the inner office door.*] Mr. Drake! Mr. Drake! It is I—Miss Sullivan! I must see you, sir!

CARTWRIGHT [*panicking*]. Hush! Don't, please! You threaten my position with this ballyhoo. I...I shall consult his appointment book. Perhaps I will find a space for you after all.

MISS SULLIVAN. It is highly advisable for you to do so, for I shan't budge from this cushion until I have spoken with Mr. Drake.

[CARTWRIGHT *paces for a moment, then goes behind his desk and stands there. He looks at* MISS SULLIVAN, *then at the inner office door.*]

MISS SULLIVAN. So, when is his next available appointment? I should prefer one before twelve o'clock, as I, too, am taking luncheon to-day.

CARTWRIGHT. I am checking. If you would only be patient.

[CARTWRIGHT *stares at her for a long moment, then takes a deep breath, reaches down and opens a desk drawer. There is the sound of heavy metallic contents rattling around.*]

CARTWRIGHT [*groping in drawer*]. I believe I have something for you, Miss Sullivan. Something definitive. Most definitive.

[*He has found what he was looking for. He holds it behind the desk and gazes at it, but neither* MISS SULLIVAN *nor the audience can see the item.*]

MISS SULLIVAN. I should hope you do. For your sake. Not to mention…

[*As she is talking, she is distracted by a man, B.A. NOYING, wearing a large sandwich board, who has entered and now stands downstage, directly in the center, blocking the audience's view of the action upstage. The sandwich board holds posters advertising the theatre company's upcoming season. Mr. NOYING also carries two signs on long sticks, which he raises as he faces the audience. These signs have over-the-top quotes from theater reviewers: e.g., "THIS THEATRE COMPANY is stupendous! Best I've ever seen! Great value! Now that's theatre!"*]

NOYING [*to audience*]. Hi there. This theatre company is proud to bring you quality productions such as *The Clean-Shaven Secretary with the Pistol*. We think you'll agree that live theater offers the best entertainment value for your dollar.

[*As he speaks, upstage* CARTWRIGHT *and* MISS SULLI-
VAN *look at each other in confusion. They drift downstage on
either side of* NOYING *to watch him.*]

NOYING. But unfortunately, in recent years ticket prices
have only enabled us to cover our minimum expenses.
This theatre company needs your additional support.
For a modest contribution of fifty dollars, you'll
receive…

[*An attractive* MODEL *walks on stage carrying a tote bag.
Each time he mentions an item, she produces it and displays
it gracefully.*]

NOYING. …this lovely tote bag. And for just fifty dollars
more, we're pleased to offer you this…

[*The* MODEL *reaches in the bag and pulls out its contents.*
CARTWRIGHT *and* MISS SULLIVAN *converge on* NOYING.]

NOYING. …Great Performances DVD and book com-
panion set. And if you act now—

MISS SULLIVAN. What the hell are you doing? We're in
the middle of a show here!

[NOYING *glances at the two actors, who glower at him.
He then launches into his pitch, talking fast so he can get it
all in.*]

NOYING. And if you act now, we'll include a terrific—

MISS SULLIVAN [*shoving him*]. Hey! Are you brain-dead,
buddy?

CARTWRIGHT. She's right. Get lost.

NOYING. Look, I'm just trying to do my job… [*Beams at audience.*] …which is to inform these wonderful theatre patrons about the fine programs we have coming up, and to remind them of how their generous contributions enable us to continue providing them with the highest quality local theatre!

[MISS SULLIVAN *wrenches one of the signs away from him and throws it. The sign slaps on the stage floor.*]

NOYING. Hey!

[*Upstage, enter* DRAKE, *looking in the direction of the desk.*]

DRAKE. My God, Cartwright! What was that?

[DRAKE *looks around the desk and sofa, sees everyone downstage and crosses quickly to them. NOTE:* DRAKE *remains in the stiff, presentational style throughout the play, not even breaking character to check out the sexy* MODEL.]

DRAKE [*in a pseudo-English accent*]. Hello? What the devil is going—

MISS SULLIVAN. Oh, shut up, Jack. Can't you break character for a second? You and Dustin Hoffman with that Method crap. Oooh, I never break character. I have to *live* my roles.

CARTWRIGHT [*pointing at* NOYING *and the* MODEL]. Hey, Jack…these two just barged onstage in the middle of our performance. It's like a commercial or something.

DRAKE. It is most irregular. [*To* NOYING.] If you do not clear the stage this instant, I shall be forced to notify the union. And there will be consequences, sir, I assure you.

MISS SULLIVAN. Yeah, that's effective. Windbag. [*To* NOYING.] Your mother must be really proud, huh? Making a living as a walking sandwich board and play interrupter? You're a joke. [*To* MODEL.] And you, honey—you're just sad. They didn't even give you a line, did they?

[*The* MODEL *forces a smile and makes gift-posing gestures.* NOYING *breaks his "pledge-drive host" character.*]

NOYING. You're being unfair. At least I'm doing my pitch in period costume, with this nice sandwich board. I mean, the producers could have decided to wheel a TV on stage. At least this way it's authentic to the period, right?

MISS SULLIVAN. Yeah, that totally makes it okay. Ass.

NOYING. Look, lady, I'm an actor, same as you. I'm just trying to make a living over here, all right? These commercial gigs pay well, and some of us can't afford to have artistic principles. We can't afford to do [*makes air quotes*] *high art* like this play, this uh… [*to* CARTWRIGHT] What's the name of this play again?

CARTWRIGHT. *The Clean Shaven Secretary with the Pistol.*

NOYING. Right—*The Clean Shaven Secretary with the Pistol*. What kind of stupid, pretentious title is that anyway?

MISS SULLIVAN. You're an idiot, you know that? Clearly you don't know a damn thing about the theatre—certainly nothing about the great Chekhov. One of his first plays had this title. It ran briefly in Saint Petersburg, but the text was lost so nobody knows what it was about. Only the title survived. This is an *homage* to Chekhov, dipshit.

NOYING. Listen, if you'll just let me finish my pitch, we can get back to your little show in five, ten minutes, tops.

MISS SULLIVAN. Ten minutes? This whole *play* is only supposed to go ten minutes, and we're already…

[CARTWRIGHT *checks his pocket watch.*]

CARTWRIGHT. Six, seven into it. No, seven. I think this is slow.

MISS SULLIVAN. Whatever. We've only got about three minutes left.

[DRAKE *steps up to the footlights, raises his chin and speaks his line loudly, as if projecting it to a sleepy usher at the back of the house.*]

DRAKE. I have warned you… [*To* NOYING, *softly.*] What is your name, sir?

NOYING. B.A. Noying.

DRAKE. Thank you. [*Resumes stiff posture, speaks loudly.*] I have warned you, Mr. Noying. I shall brook this intrusion no longer! I will return with the board or union management.

[DRAKE *exits*.]

CARTWRIGHT [*to* NOYING]. You're really screwing us, here, you know that? This was a good part for me. [*Scans the audience.*] I just hope my agent isn't here tonight.

MISS SULLIVAN [*right in* NOYING's *face*]. You—*you* are what's killing art. [*Waves an arm at the audience.*] All they care about is what was going to happen when Cartwright was rummaging in the desk. That's *it*. But you knew that, didn't you? You advertising pukes always know. You know exactly when to interrupt. You wait for the perfect moment, the moment of highest suspense, and then you barge in with your smiles and your "hi there's" and whatever product you're peddling, and no matter where we go or what we do, we can't get away from you, because you're everywhere—like dust. [*Gazing into the distance in a trance.*] We turn on the TV and you come on, blaring twice as loud as the show we were just watching. We put on a DVD and you're there, too, and we can't even fast-forward to the movie because you sneaky pricks disabled the option. Or we go to the movies, only to discover you've infected those as well. Except now the 30-second ads for cars or soda are five minutes long. But you don't care. You've got us. We're literally being held captive. You're on signs, in cabs, in elevators, at gas stations, on our phones and computer screens—you're even in our bathrooms, for God's sake! Guys go to urinals, and the little rubber splash guards have ads on them. [*To* Noying.] Well, guess what? Not tonight. Uh-uh, not my show. You're not finishing your pitch. In fact, I'm going to use the remaining time to cut to the chase, to tell the audience the rest of the story. [*Turns to audience.*] So, Miss Sullivan enters—that's me—and demands to see Mr. Drake. Cartwright is very upset, and when I demand to see Drake, Cartwright goes to his desk. Supposedly to check the appointment book, but he's actually looking for something else. He's looking for—

[The Playwright *enters. He storms on stage, followed by* Drake, *who remains in character. The* Model *drifts over to the others and stands near* Cartwright.]

Playwright. *What* is going on? You're ruining my play!

Model. Who is that?

Cartwright. Nobody. Just the playwright.

[Miss Sullivan *sidles up to the* Playwright.]

Miss Sullivan [*points at* Noying *and the* Model]. They hijacked your show. I tried to stop them. Believe me, I *love* your words, and I would never do anything to desecrate them.

Playwright. I want you two off. Now.

Noying. I am contracted to be here.

MISS SULLIVAN. Beat it!

[*She* throws her stuffed dog at NOYING. *The* PLAYWRIGHT *picks up the fallen sign and starts beating him with it.*]

NOYING [*quickly to audience; cowering*]. Folks, for more information, go to this theater's website! Ow! Or call 1-800-GO-THEATER. Ow! Operators are standing by. We need your support! Ow! Thank you!

[*The* PLAYWRIGHT *drives* NOYING *and the* MODEL *offstage.*]

MODEL. Eeek!

NOYING [*offstage*]. Ow! Come on already. Stop it!

[*The three actors still on stage stare at each other and nod simultaneously.* MISS SULLIVAN *and* DRAKE *run offstage to their original entry points.* CARTWRIGHT *resumes his place behind the desk, straightening papers and humming his tune—but much faster this time. NOTE: Everything he and* MISS SULLIVAN *do now—the first two 2-3 minutes of the play, with some dialogue clipped or compressed—is performed as though they are on fast-forward.* CARTWRIGHT *crosses to the outer office door and whips out his pocket watch. His hand hovers over the lock.*]

CARTWRIGHT. And…now!

[*He opens the door and steps aside as* MISS SULLIVAN *enters.*]

CARTWRIGHT. Good morning. Wh—what are you doing here?

[*She breezes past him and stands near his desk.*]

MISS SULLIVAN. I demand to see Mr. Drake!

CARTWRIGHT. I am afraid that is impossible. Mr. Drake is busy this morning. All morning.

MISS SULLIVAN [*sitting down*]. Then I shall wait here. I shall wait all day if necessary. I will be heard, Mr. Cartwright.

CARTWRIGHT. Sorry. Mr. Drake takes luncheon at one o'clock, and meetings and appointments will occupy him this afternoon. [*He crosses to her, takes her gloved hand.*] Go home. I'll give you cab fare.

MISS SULLIVAN [*yanking her hand away*]. Cab fare? Cab fare! I will not be silenced for such a paltry sum. [*Loudly, towards the inner office door.*] Mr. Drake! It's me—Miss Sullivan! I must see you, sir!

CARTWRIGHT [*panicking*]. Stop! I'll check his appointment book. Maybe I can find a space for you.

MISS SULLIVAN. I should hope so, for I shan't budge from this cushion until I have spoken with Mr. Drake.

[CARTWRIGHT *paces like a cartoon character, then goes behind his desk and stands there. Tapping his foot, he looks at* MISS SULLIVAN, *then at the inner office door.*]

MISS SULLIVAN. When is his next available appointment? Before twelve o'clock is preferable, as I, too, am taking luncheon to-day.

CARTWRIGHT. Hold your horses, I'm checking.

[CARTWRIGHT *stares at her for a long moment, then reaches down and opens a desk drawer. There is the sound of heavy contents rattling as he gropes around.*]

CARTWRIGHT. I believe I have something for you. Something definitive. Most definitive.

[*He has found what he was looking for. But as raises it up behind the desk...*]

CARTWRIGHT. Hold it! Hold it!

[*He drops whatever was in his hand back into the desk drawer, closes it, and stands up holding the pocket watch.*]

CARTWRIGHT. That's ten minutes. Maybe eleven. We're out of time.

[DRAKE *enters. He is still in character.*]

DRAKE. Oh, this is most disappointing. I intend to lodge a complaint.

MISS SULLIVAN [*sighs, glares at* DRAKE]. God I hate you.

END OF PLAY

Dark and Stormy Night

CHARACTERS

NORA: An attractive waitress. Mid-late 20s. Long hair in braids.

SHANLEY: A caretaker/poet in his 30s. Looks like an L.L. Bean model.

STATE TROOPER: Wears the signature hat. Late 50s, nearing retirement.

JUNKIE: Young man with scraggly hair and unkempt clothing.

SETTING

The interior of a diner on a desolate road.

TIME

An autumn night. The present.

THE SCENE

The diner is empty, except one booth. Here, the lone waitress, Nora, *sips coffee and reads the novel* Anna Karenina. *It's late and nearing the end of her shift. Over the traditional waitress outfit of a black skirt and white blouse,* Nora *wears a bright red cardigan. She glances out the window at the loud and slashing rain.* Nora *slowly zips her thumb along the six or seven hundred pages she has yet to read.*

Nora. Ugh. Russians.

[Nora *hears a car or notices headlights outside. She marks her place in the book and straightens her braids in the window reflection. The door opens and a soaked attractive man,* Shanley, *walks in with a splitting maul over his shoulder. Silent, he grabs a fistful of napkins from a dispenser, hesitates for a moment, grabs some more, and begins to meticulously dry off…the maul and its handle.*]

Nora. Hey, woodsman—maybe you'd prefer a towel? You know, save a tree?

Shanley. These are fine. Thanks.

Nora. I could put it in the oven for you. I think it'll fit.

[Shanley *ignores her. He finishes drying the maul and leans it against the counter like an umbrella, then sits on a stool at the counter.*]

Nora. Listen, should I be worried?

Shanley. Excuse me?

NORA. Oh, you know…guy walks in out of the rain, middle of nowhere, with an axe. A few scary movies have started that way.

SHANLEY. Yeah? Which ones?

NORA. Like *Friday the 13th*, I think.

SHANLEY. Maybe. But this is a splitting maul, not an axe.

NORA. Splits stuff in half, doesn't it? Close enough. [*She gazes out the window.*] It was a dark and stormy night. Ah…good ole' Snoopy.

SHANLEY. What about Snoopy?

NORA. You know, his writing. Every time he started a novel, he'd open with that stormy night business. Didn't you ever read *Peanuts*?

SHANLEY. Never liked comics. Never thought they were funny. Too forced. "Hey, kids, it's Sunday morning—time to laugh!"

NORA. Well, like my grandfather used to say, you got a right. So…what can I getcha? Besides napkins for your little friend. Cook left an hour ago, so nothing hot.

SHANLEY. That include the coffee?

NORA. See it steaming over there?

SHANLEY. Coffee then. Black. And coconut cream pie if you've got it.

NORA. I don't. Only pumpkin and blueberry.

SHANLEY. Somebody ruined blueberry pie for me. All right…pumpkin. Pumpkin.

NORA. Ha, ha.

SHANLEY. And the coffee.

[NORA *whisks away, pours the coffee, slices the pie. As her back is turned,* SHANLEY *looks around suspiciously.* NORA *returns with the food.*]

NORA. Anything else?

SHANLEY. I'll text you.

NORA. Can't. No phone.

SHANLEY. Me either.

NORA. We must be the only two in America.

SHANLEY. Must be.

[NORA *walks away for a moment while* SHANLEY *eats. She returns with her coffee and sits on the stool next to his.*]

NORA. So, you never answered my question.

SHANLEY. What question?

NORA. Should I be worried? [*She taps the maul handle.*] Guys who walk around with these tend not to be what you'd call…*stable.*

SHANLEY. Look, my truck lock's broken. I've had this a long time and I don't want some crackhead stealing it.

NORA. Lot of maul thefts where you're from?

SHANLEY. Forget the maul. What about you? What's your story?

NORA. I work here. I don't need a story.

SHANLEY. You see, I think you do. And I think you've got a good one. Pretty girl, working late, reading Tolstoy. What is that, *War and Peace*, or the other one?

NORA. The other one.

SHANLEY. So you crave romance. You married? Don't tell me…you're bored and want a handsome Vronsky on the side.

NORA. Omigod, you've read it?

SHANLEY. Damn right I've read it. Just because a man has a splitting maul doesn't mean he's ignorant. You prejudged me, missy. So…you…either you're not married or—since I don't see a ring—you're married and poor. I'm going to guess…not married. But there's a boyfriend. Local woodchuck, probably out with his buddies right now, drinking Busch and shooting road signs. Am I right?

NORA. Everything except shooting road signs. He's not that ambitious.

SHANLEY. You've got some education, right?

NORA. A degree in English lit. I know—totally useless.

SHANLEY. How the hell did you end up here?

NORA. How does anybody end up anywhere? It just happens. Imperceptibly, like a glacier. Actually, I like to cross-country ski. I was team captain.

SHANLEY. You Norwegian?

NORA. My mother's side, why?

SHANLEY. Nobody does cross-country like those Norwegians. And exciting? My God, when the Olympics are on, and they're coming down the home stretch, I'm shouting at the TV: "Come on! Move your Norwegian asses! Move!"

NORA. You're teasing me. You think cross-country is stupid.

SHANLEY. No, I think it *looks* stupid. But I admire the athletes.

[*He looks at her for a long moment, then fingers one of her braids.*]

SHANLEY. What's with the Laura Ingalls getup?

NORA. Hey, watch it. I happen to love *Little House*.

SHANLEY. I didn't say it was unattractive.

NORA [*pulls her braid away, spins on the stool*]. So, a splitting maul, huh? You must be a real man's man.

SHANLEY. Actually, I'm better than that. I'm a man's man's man.

Nora [*laughs*]. All right, compared to you, where do the real manly men rank? Guys like Clint Eastwood or Anthony Quinn.

Shanley. Towelboys in a Turkish bathhouse, my dear. Towelboys.

[*He pushes his plate away.*]

Nora. Didn't like your pie?

[Shanley *shrugs.*]

Nora. More coffee?

Shanley. No, but I'd like something else.

[Shanley *turns* Nora *so she faces him. Then, gently taking hold of her braids, he eases her mouth towards his. Their lips barely touch when they hear a car outside.* Nora *pulls away and stands up.*]

Nora. This'll just take a sec.

[Nora *produces a cup carrier from beneath the counter and pours coffee into cups.* Shanley *looks outside, picks up the splitting maul and starts offstage.*]

Nora. Where you going?

Shanley. Bathroom.

[Shanley *exits. A* State Trooper *enters, water dripping from his hat brim.*]

State Trooper. Evening, Nora. The usual. And two extras, black.

Nora. Way ahead of you.

State Trooper. Advantage of being a regular.

Nora. Bad out there tonight, huh?

State Trooper. Yeah, lot of limbs down. Not a night to be driving around, that's for sure. Kind of weather that brings out the crazies. Anybody suspicious come in tonight?

Nora. No, why?

State Trooper. Experience. Dark and stormy night like this, weird stuff tends to happen. It's not just in the movies. Don't mean to worry you, Nora, but you *are* alone here. Got our number, right?

[*She hands him the finished cup carrier.*]

Nora. I do.

State Trooper. Well, don't be afraid to use it. What do I owe you?

Nora. On the house. Stay safe. I'll be fine.

State Trooper. Evening then.

[*The* State Trooper *exits back into the storm.* Nora *looks outside until the car is gone.*]

Nora [*loudly*]. Okay…you can come out now!

[SHANLEY *enters.*]

SHANLEY. Were you calling to me?

NORA. State Trooper just left.

SHANLEY. Trooper? What'd he want?

NORA. Asked me if I'd seen any suspicious characters in here tonight. Told him no. I didn't tell him you were here, in case you were wondering.

SHANLEY. I wasn't, and I wouldn't care if you had. Besides, when he said suspicious, I think he meant people like this guy.

[*The door bangs open and a* JUNKIE *stumbles inside. He has scraggly hair, long sideburns and a thick beard. He shakes involuntarily and looks warily around the diner.*]

NORA. All right, what can I getcha? We're about to close.

[*The* JUNKIE *shuffles over to the counter and stands across from* NORA. *He reaches in his pocket and pulls out a comically small knife.*]

JUNKIE. You can get me all the money from that register, sweetcakes, that's what.

NORA. Sweetcakes? What's a sweetcake? And what's that thing in your hand?

JUNKIE. It's a knife, what do you think?

NORA. A paring knife? Come on. If you're gonna rob places, at least get a good knife.

Junkie. Are you giving me the money or not?

Nora. Normally I wouldn't. But you I feel sorry for.

[*Before* Nora *can open the register,* Shanley *steps in front of the* Junkie *and drops the maul head on the counter, making the coffee cups jump. The* Junkie *scurries backward and flashes the knife around.*]

Junkie. Watch it, buddy, I've got a knife!

Shanley. Splitting maul. Maul trumps knife, junior.

Junkie. You don't scare me with that. I could stab you like thirty times before you even picked it up.

[*The* Junkie *dances in a circle, slashing and stabbing as though single-handedly fighting off the entire Sharks gang from* West Side Story. *Meanwhile,* Shanley *methodically takes the cover off the donut tray and places a cruller on a stool.*]

Shanley. Hey, kid. I want to show you something.

[*The* Junkie *freezes.* Shanley *assumes his wood-splitting stance, winds up, and brings the maul down with a loud crash on the cruller, cleaving it perfectly in half. He tosses one half of the cruller to the* Junkie.]

Shanley. Now get lost, kid.

[*The* Junkie, *nibbling the cruller, backs up to the door and leaves.*]

Nora. Wow, you *are* good with that thing, aren't you? I was just gonna give him the money.

[SHANLEY *finishes the cruller and sips some coffee.*]

SHANLEY. So, is this what you plan on doing for the rest of your life?

NORA. What do you mean?

SHANLEY. Oh, let's see…living with somebody you can't stand, working a job you can't stand, reading books you can't discuss with anybody, getting robbed by drug addicts? Isn't that a waste?

NORA. Well, what alternative do I have? In case you haven't noticed, opportunities aren't exactly plentiful around here.

SHANLEY. Maybe *I'm* an opportunity. Maybe I'm a chance for you to get out of this place.

NORA. Maybe you're an axe murderer.

SHANLEY. Only one way to find out.

[NORA *takes a long look around the diner. After standing still for some time, she gets her book and purse from the booth, clears their dishes and shuts out the kitchen lights.*]

NORA. This is insane.

SHANLEY. No more insane than staying here the rest of your life and expecting things to change. [*He puts the maul over his shoulder.*] Somebody once said that insanity is doing the same thing over and over, expecting a different result.

NORA. Yeah, but what if the guy who said that was insane? [*She nods at the splitting maul.*] You better not kill me.

[*They kiss.*]

SHANLEY. I'm Shanley by the way.

NORA. Nora. I need to stop at my apartment and get a few things. Books mostly.

SHANLEY. Of course.

NORA. So who ruined blueberry pie for you? And more important, how?

[*They walk out with their arms around each other.*]

END OF PLAY

FRONT PAGE ABOVE THE FOLD

CHARACTERS

DIANE: The city editor. A middle-aged professional woman, exasperated by her reporters. Wears a watch.

JOSIE: The charismatic, extroverted Ace Reporter. Smartly dressed, she has a quick, all-business gait.

LOUISE: The weary workhorse reporter. Pitches and writes more stories than all the others. Wears glasses.

BOB: One half of the Bob/Carl investigative reporting duo. They dress exactly the same and gesture in tandem.

CARL: The second half of the Bob/Carl investigative reporting duo. They dress exactly the same and gesture in tandem.

BROCK: The newspaper's golden boy. Prefers press releases to digging for stories. Gets away with a lot because he's so damn good-looking.

SETTING

A conference room at the *Poughkeepsie Journal*, a daily newspaper in the city of Poughkeepsie, NY.

TIME

Present day.

THE SCENE

A conference room in the venerable newspaper's office. It's the daily meeting between reporters and the editor, when the reporters pitch their stories for the next day's paper. The city editor, Diane, sits alone impatiently checking her watch and the door. A moment later Josie sashays in.

Josie. Hullo, Diane! Have I got a story for you! It's got it all, I tell you. Danger, drama, and a dog. And it *bleeds*, Diane. And you know the old saying—if it bleeds, it leads. [*Dreamily.*] I can see it now. Front page above the fold.

Diane. You're late, Josie. Again.

Josie. Yes, but for good reason, Diane. I was having breakfast at the diner with my cop buddies, and they were giving me the scoop. I'm like their kid sister.

Diane. What's the story?

Josie. Rocky the Rabid Raccoon Killer.

Diane. Excuse me?

Josie. You know the problems we've had with rabid raccoons in the area.

Diane. Of course.

Josie. Well, Rocky's a German Shepherd that's killed three of them. The last one he killed was about to attack a toddler playing in the park. Rocky swooped in and saved the little girl.

DIANE. And where did Rocky kill these raccoons?

JOSIE. Poughkeepsie.

DIANE. Hmm. City or town?

JOSIE. That's the beauty, Diane. Both. Two in the town and one right here in the city! And I've got art! Rocky with a raccoon in his jaws.

DIANE. People do love dogs.

JOSIE. You bet. Especially hero dogs. Like, remember the story we ran—the one about the dog that woke up its owners when the house was on fire? This'll dwarf that one in popularity. Nobody likes rabid raccoons. Nobody.

DIANE. That's for sure. Not bad, Josie.

JOSIE. What'd you expect? I wasn't nominated for a Pulitzer for nothing.

[DIANE *checks her watch;* JOSIE *glances at the door.*]

DIANE. You're looking a little tired, Josie. Hope you're not burning the candle at both ends.

JOSIE. Oh, you know me, Diane—busy, busy.

DIANE. Because—and maybe it's not my place to say this—I don't think it's wise for you to be spending so much time with Brock.

JOSIE. How did you...?

DIANE. A good editor sees everything, Josie. Comma splices, dangling modifiers, and doomed relationships. Just be careful, that's all I'm saying.

[LOUISE *enters.*]

DIANE [*taps her watch*]. Louise.

LOUISE. Sorry. I was down in payroll, trying to get my mileage reimbursement. I've been after them for a month. I wish you'd talk to them, Diane.

DIANE. I'll see what I can do. Just once I'd like to be able to start on time. Where are the boys? Anybody know?

LOUISE. Last I saw, Bob and Carl were on the phone, and Brock was sipping coffee at his desk.

[BOB *and* CARL *enter.*]

DIANE. Late and late. And speaking of late, you two still owe me that story on the deer-culling aftermath. Where is it?

BOB. We're polishing it.

CARL. Yeah, polishing it.

DIANE. *Polishing.* That means I'll never see it. Josie?

JOSIE. Yeah?

DIANE. Get the notes from these clowns and give me ten inches on the protesters.

JOSIE. On it.

DIANE. Make sure you write a solid nutgraph about why they had to cull the deer in the first place. [*She snaps her fingers.*] Maybe interview that lady with the crazy hair. You know—the one who claims to have had Lyme disease eleven times?

LOUISE. Eleven times? Lady, stay out of the woods already. Yeesh.

[BROCK *enters.*]

JOSIE. Hey, Brock. Late night?

BROCK. Something like that.

DIANE. Okay, people, I have my meeting with Stan in five minutes and I have lots of column inches to fill. I need your stories. Who's got our lead?

LOUISE. Hey, Brock was late, too! Where's his reprimand?

DIANE. I'll hear his story pitch first.

BROCK. Look no further, Diane. I've got your headline. The Hudson Valley Renegades are sending a pitcher to the show. This is big news.

LOUISE. Big sports news maybe.

CARL. So they're sending a guy up to the majors. So *what*?

BROCK. So...the kid's only got one arm. He's a one-armed pitcher.

BOB [*claps halfheartedly*]. Stellar reporting there, Brock. Real tough reading a press release. Besides, the one-armed pitcher thing's been done to death. Now, if it were a one-legged pitcher, that would impress me. Then you'd have something.

JOSIE. I think it's great, Brock.

DIANE. Bob's got a point. I feel like I've seen this story before. Next.

LOUISE. The Nobel laureate for Literature is doing a reading at—

JOSIE. Yawn. Nobody cares about the arts.

LOUISE. Okay. Well, there's been talk of Westchester seceding from New York. Seems they want to join Connecticut.

CARL. Two words. Let 'em.

BROCK. So…as you're probably aware, there's been a national backlash against standardized testing lately.

BOB. Big deal. We've heard this before. Some high school brats don't want to take the SATs. Boo hoo.

BROCK. Actually, this involves elementary kids. The other day apparently, a bunch of fourth-graders over in Millbrook walked out of the CTBS tests. Fourth graders.

DIANE. Page one Mid-Hudson section. Maybe.

[*There's a pause as the reporters look at each other to see who goes next.*]

LOUISE. This could be something. Half the state assembly is backing a bill that legalizes cage fighting.

JOSIE. Please. How is this different from the brawls they already have up there? Pass it, I say. Let them beat each other to death.

CARL. We should be so lucky.

DIANE. What else?

LOUISE. How about this? There's been grumbling in the county legislature about overcrowding in the jail, and now there's a proposal to fix it.

DIANE. Go on.

LOUISE. Well, up to now the talk has been about building a bigger jail. But the county simply doesn't have the money. So the latest idea is something they're calling the Adopt-an-Inmate Program. County residents who agree to house and feed an inmate will get a tax break.

DIANE. If they pass legislation to that effect, we'll run it. Brock, what about you? Anything else?

BROCK. Why me? I just pitched half a dozen stories.

DIANE. No, you pitched two.

BROCK. Fine. I was thinking of a follow-up piece on the redevelopment of the old mental hospital on Route 9. It's been a year since they proposed that mental health museum and theme park.

DIANE. And what makes it news?

BROCK. It's a hundred million dollar proposal and they're dragging their feet. That's the news.

CARL. Somebody's on the take there.

DIANE [to CARL and BOB]. Why is everything a conspiracy with you two? Did your parents forget to pick you up on your first day of school? What's your damage?

[BOB and CARL look at each other and shrug simultaneously.]

DIANE. It's weak, Brock. Tomorrow's lead story needs substance.

CARL. We've got substance.

BOB. We've got substance.

DIANE. Okay, I'll bite. But this better be good.

BOB. One word…Arterialgate.

DIANE. Explain.

CARL. Well, Diane, as you know, Bob and I have been investigating the timing of the traffic lights on the Arterial.

DIANE. Refresh my memory. What's the issue?

BOB. Simple—how you can never get all the way through Poughkeepsie without hitting a red light. We've tried it at every speed—30, 33, 35—it doesn't matter. We've driven as slow as 25 and as fast as 50, and we've never made it all the way through without hitting a red light. We've tried it on the hour and the half-hour. We've tried it days, nights, and the wee hours of the morning. We've tried it on weekdays, weekends, holidays—

CARL. I'm telling you it's a conspiracy! And we're going to prove it!

DIANE. Who are your sources?

CARL. We've been talking with a former city planner who was around when they created the Arterial, and he told us that they specifically timed the lights to trap drivers in the city. But that's on deep background. Our source isn't willing to come forward. He's afraid of retribution.

DIANE. Damn it, when is somebody going to go on the record in this story!? [*She sighs.*] All right. Have I heard everybody's pitch?

LOUISE. We haven't heard Josie's.

CARL. That's right. We haven't.

JOSIE [*waggles a pen, or some other business*]. Rocky the Rabid Raccoon Killer.

CARL. That's it?

JOSIE. Yup. Diane's already heard it. She knows the angle.

BROCK. Hard to beat, kid.

JOSIE. Thank you, Brock.

BROCK [*aside to* JOSIE]. See you tonight, babe?

Josie [*aside to* Brock]. Counting the minutes, ace.

Bob. Wait, is this about that dog that killed those rabid raccoons? You've got to be kidding me.

Louise. For once I agree with Bob. You want the front page story? I've got a Nobel laureate, county secession, cage fighting, and an Adopt-an-Inmate Program. Take your pick.

Bob. To hell with those. We've got a city-wide conspiracy.

Carl [*glaring around the room*]. Maybe even *state*-wide.

Josie. Diane's right—everything's a conspiracy with you two. Get off it already.

Carl. Yeah? Well maybe you ought to get off of Brock.

Josie. What!

Bob. Especially since Brock can't get off of Stacy from Layout.

Josie. What!

Carl. We saw the two of you last night—at *Shadows*—hanging all over each other. It's disgusting.

Josie [*to* Brock]. Stacy. From Layout? Layout, Brock? Layout?

Brock. Wait a second. [*To* Bob *and* Carl.] Have you been following me? That's really creepy, guys.

Louise. I second that.

JOSIE. Mind your own business, Louise.

[*The scene EXPLODES into an argument, with the reporters ad-libbing personal insults at each other.*]

DIANE. People. People! Enough! Pull yourselves together. You're journalists for God's sake. Have a little dignity. You write for the *Poughkeepsie Journal.* Remember that. This is New York's oldest newspaper. You're part of a long and noble tradition going back to 1785. This paper reported on the ratification of the Bill of Rights. We were here when Alexander Hamilton was killed in a duel, and we were here when the Civil War broke out. We got through the Great Depression and countless recessions, and we did it by reporting on the news that matters. The Moon Landing. The end of the Cold War. Big events. Important events. We've been here for over 200 years, and God willing we'll be here for another 200—or at least as long as people read newspapers. So, what am I saying? Be proud of the paper you write for. Compose yourselves. Have some dignity.

[*The reporters all sit up straighter, with proud expressions on their faces. They look at each other and nod.*]

DIANE. I've got to get to my meeting.

LOUISE. Wait—Diane—front page above the fold. Which story gets it?

DIANE. Rocky the Rabid Raccoon Killer of course. We've gotta sell some papers, don't we?

END OF PLAY

Microbrew

CHARACTERS

P.F.: Unemployed civil engineer in his early 20s; tall, heavyset, wears glasses and a rock concert T-shirt.

ALEX: Handsome young waiter, also early 20s; wears sandals and a safari shirt.

JUNE: 89-year-old grandmother of P.F.; wears gardening clothes and a huge straw hat.

SETTING

A flower garden in front of a large Victorian home. The house's porch and door are in the background.

TIME

A spring afternoon. Mid-1990s.

THE SCENE

An old woman, June, *kneels in front of a flower bed, digging and weeding. She wears a giant straw hat. In the background is a porch, badly in need of painting. P.F. and* Alex *are heading toward the porch when they spot* June.

Alex. Crap.

P.F. Put the beer in the bushes.

Alex. But it'll skunk.

P.F. In the bushes. I don't feel like getting the third degree.

[*The two walk over to* June.]

P.F. Hey, June.

Alex. She didn't hear you.

June. Course I heard him. Also heard him when he told you to hide the hooch. [*To* P.F.] He's right, you know. Better get it before it skunks.

[P.F. *retrieves the paper bag of beer.*]

June. Stand in the light you two, where I can see you. [*Clucks her tongue.*] Gaining weight, boys. Drinking too much of that damn beer. [*Digging in the dirt.*] Back in'28, I went with a boy who liked the brew. Got fatter'n the Michelin Man. The cirrhosis took him in '39. Damn shame.

Alex. That's rough.

P.F. Need us to do something for you, June?

JUNE. I'd ask you to paint the porch, but you'd never do it. You two working now or what?

ALEX. I am.

JUNE. Doing what?

ALEX. Waiting tables.

JUNE. Can't pay much.

ALEX. The money's pretty good, actually. I'm writing a book, too.

JUNE. Got a publisher?

ALEX. No.

JUNE. Then what the hell you writing it for, no one's gonna read it?

ALEX. They might. Besides, it's more for me. I like the process.

JUNE. What process?

ALEX. The writing process.

JUNE. *Process.* Time was, a man did a job to get paid. [*Gestures at* P.F. *with a garden tool.*] What about you?

P.F. Not working right now, June. Probably going back to school.

JUNE. School? You just got four years of that. To do what?

P.F. Get my master's. Zymurgy.

JUNE. Zymurgy?! What the hell is that?

P.F. It's a science, June. Brewing.

JUNE. Makin' *beer*? You're going back to school for that? You can make beer right in the basement. Don't need another degree.

P.F. I'm already doing that.

ALEX. He's made some really good ales, June. Your grandson has a gift.

P.F. Well, gift might be a bit strong. I'm not curing cancer with the stuff.

ALEX. Not yet.

JUNE. Got a gift, does he? Also got an engineering degree that cost his father a hundred grand.

P.F. Brewing's a lot more sophisticated today, June. Microbrews are popping up all over the place. Couple years from now, I could be a millionaire.

JUNE. What the heck's a microbrew?

P.F. Well, they're beers made in smaller batches. The breweries are a lot more efficient than the big guys— you know, like Coors or Anheuser-Busch. And they use better quality ingredients, so they can make better-tasting beer and charge more for it. Some cities, like Seattle and Portland, they've got half a dozen of these microbrews. [*To* ALEX.] Give her one of the Dock Street.

JUNE. Too early for drinking.

P.F. It's one beer, June. Trust me, you've never had a Pilsner like this one.

[ALEX *opens one with the convenient bottle opener on his keychain and hands the beer to* JUNE. *She takes a sip, smacks her lips and nods.*]

JUNE. Gotta admit—refreshing. Not bitter at all. Lot tastier than the brew I remember.

P.F. That's the hops. It's easier to get the good stuff today.

JUNE. Your brother Billy's doing well. Maybe he can get you a job with the shtate.

ALEX. The 'shtate'?

P.F. She means the State Department of Transportation. June…Billy's married and everything. He likes that kind of work. I don't.

JUNE. Drove by the office yesterday. Hiring a lot of people, looks like. You boys should go on up there, put in an application. All the young fellas are linin' up!

P.F. Maybe we will.

ALEX. I don't know what job I'd do, but maybe.

JUNE. You could be one of those fellas with the flag. I hear they make twenty-five an hour. That's good money. Better'n you're making now, I bet.

ALEX. On average, yes.

[JUNE *sets her bottle on the ground.*]

P.F. Good, right?

JUNE. Not bad. You said you made some of your own. Got any around?

P.F. Sure!

[P.F. *exits.*]

ALEX. This is really making his day, June.

JUNE. I haven't had a beer in the middle of the day since…oh, must've been summer of '28. Wish I could remember that boy's name.

ALEX. You're sassy, June. The boys must have been buzzing around you nonstop.

JUNE. Bet your ass they did. And I could drink any of 'em under the table.

ALEX. You think you would have liked me?

JUNE. Oh, sure. You're a looker. But you couldn't of handled me. I was wild. Wild.

ALEX. I don't know. I've been with some pretty wild girls.

JUNE. I once arm-wrestled Al Smith and beat him.

ALEX. Who's Al Smith?

JUNE. Damn your generation doesn't know squat! New York Governor, ran for President. I was working a booth at the county fair. He made some crack—can't remember what—and before I knew it we were arm-wrestling. Little fella. Short arms, that was his trouble.

ALEX. Wow. How'd you get so strong, June?

JUNE. Grew up poor on a farm. You got strong or you died. That simple. [*Looking around.*] Where's that grandson of mine? Coulda brewed my own by now.

ALEX. Trust me, June…it's worth the wait. Here he is.

[*P.F. enters, carrying a quart-sized bottle of beer and three glasses. He hands ALEX and JUNE each a glass and pours the beer.*]

ALEX [*to P.F.*]. Which one'd you get?

P.F. The honey ale.

JUNE. Look out liver, look out gums. Open the hatch, 'cause here she comes!

[*The three drink simultaneously. As JUNE drinks, she looks at her glass with a surprised expression, then drinks some more.*]

P.F. Well?

Alex. Never had beer like this, have you, June?

June. *You* made this?

P.F. Yup.

June. This why you keep failing that professional engineer exam?

P.F. Yup.

June. And you say these microbrews make a lot of money.

P.F. Well, they can if their beer's good.

June [*to* Alex]. How's his compare to other stuff out there? Honest now.

Alex. Considering he's only read one book on the subject, I think he's awesome. You know that movie *The Natural?*

June. Nope.

Alex. Well, there's this amazing baseball player in it— Roy Hobbs. What Roy Hobbs is to baseball, your grandson could be to brewing. He's a natural.

June [*to* P.F.]. Come to think of it, you never showed much interest in building. Why'd you go to school for engineering anyway? What your father wanted, wasn't it?

P.F. I didn't figure out I liked brewing till senior year. By then it was too late.

[JUNE *finishes her glass and shakes her head.*]

JUNE. Don't know what secret ingredient you're using, but this beer has got me thinking, boys. All my life I played it safe. All my life I worked jobs I hated because I felt I had to, felt I didn't have a choice. Now I'm at the end. Might get another year—five if I'm lucky—and I want to do something with the time I got left. Maybe I can't handle my liquor like I used to, but the truth is you've always been my favorite grandson. I admire you for failing that engineer exam—how many times?

P.F. Seven.

JUNE. Seven?

P.F. Yeah.

JUNE. Okay, seven, so what? To hell with it. World's got enough damn engineers. What we need is more great stuff, like this beer of yours. So let me ask you, what would it take for you to start one of these microbrews?

P.F. I don't understand.

JUNE. Capital, sonny. Money to start a microbrew of your own.

P.F. I have no idea. I figured I'd get a zymurgy degree and go work for a brewery. Never thought of starting my own.

JUNE. Boys, if there's one thing I learned in life, experience is the best teacher. You want to learn how to run a microbrew, you start one. Your grandfather left me with a good chunk of dough. Time I did something constructive with it.

P.F. Your retirement money? I don't know, June. If it failed…

JUNE. So don't fail, numbnuts! Do your homework. Talk to fellas that've been successful with these microbrews. Besides, who do you think you're talking to? I lived through the Great Depression. I built B-29's during the war. And before all of that I was plain poor. I ate beans once, I can do it again.

P.F. But we're talking more than a few pennies, June. Couple hundred thousand, I'd say. At least.

JUNE [*slaps her thigh*]. Pennies, that's it! Pennyroyal. Harry Pennyroyal. That was the name of my beau, the one that died in '39.

ALEX. Pennyroyal. You know, that'd be a cool name for the company. The Pennyroyal Brewing Company. Be a nice tribute to June's boyfriend, too.

JUNE. He did love the brew. [*To* P.F.] So, how about it?

[P.F. *pours the rest of the beer into their glasses and raises his.*]

P.F. To the Pennyroyal Brewing Company.

ALEX. Getting people ripped since 1995.

[*They clink glasses, drink and sit quietly for a moment.*]

JUNE. We'll go see my lawyer tomorrow. Right now, I need a nap. Give an old lady a hand.

[P.F. *and* ALEX *each take one of her arms and walk her to the porch door.* P.F. *kisses her cheek as she walks inside.*]

P.F. Thanks, June.

JUNE. Start doing your homework. I'm not investing my money in a couple of two-bit slackers.

P.F. All right.

[*The door closes.* P.F. *and* ALEX *stand on the porch.*]

ALEX. Holy crap, right?

P.F. Yeah.

ALEX. She's serious about this?

P.F. Must be. I've never heard her talk like that.

ALEX. I guess when they reach a certain age, they don't bullshit anymore.

P.F. No time for it.

ALEX. Your own brewery! Beats linin' up with the fellas.

P.F. That's for sure.

ALEX. What now? Should we go to the library and do some research?

P.F. We could.

ALEX. Or we could wait till tomorrow, make sure it wasn't a bunch of drunk talk.

P.F. I've got a couple of home brewing magazines upstairs.

ALEX. How about we read those while drinking a few? That's research.

P.F. I do have that porter I've been waiting to try.

[*The two exit, leaving the glasses and empty beer bottles on the ground.*]

END OF PLAY

KANSAS CITY THIS IS
FORMER AIR FORCE ONE

CHARACTERS

Cooper: Chief Flight Steward Master Sergeant Cooper Jones. In his 40s. Wears a dark blue apron over the shirt, tie and slacks of a U.S. Air Force uniform.

Nixon: President Richard M. Nixon. Wearing a dark blue suit and red-white-and-blue striped tie.

Mrs. Nixon: The President's wife, Pat. Bouffant hairdo, wearing a double-knit pantsuit.

Mary: Chef Technical Sergeant Mary Knight. Chef's outfit.

Agent (Secret Service): A big man in his 30s or 40s. Talks into his jacket sleeve a lot.

Pilot: Air Force Colonel. Silver-haired, 50s.

SETTING

Aboard the Presidential 707, Air Force One: the galley, the sitting room, a crawl space. NOTE: In the galley and sitting room scenes, characters enter and exit stage left and stage right via an imaginary plane corridor that runs the entire length of downstage.

TIME

August 9, 1974. During the couple of hours that Nixon was aboard Air Force One and still President (until noon EST).

SCENE ONE

The galley of Air Force One. COOPER *and* MARY *stand at a counter, cutting pineapple. A big bowl already brims with pineapple, yet several more with their spiky tops festoon the counter. A large red fire extinguisher stands on the floor behind them. The two frequently dab their brows with their shirt sleeves because it's stifling onboard.*

MARY. Of all the days. Hotter than a Bayou swamp in here, Coop.

COOPER. What do you want me to do about it?

MARY. Nothing. Just saying—hoo, is he gonna be pissed. Why'd they get the call late?

[*The Secret Service* AGENT *walks across downstage in the imaginary corridor, whispering into his sleeve.*]

AGENT. Rhubarb, rhubarb, rhubarb, rhubarb.

MARY. Here comes your favorite person.

COOPER. God, I hope he goes with the President.

AGENT [*entering the galley*]. What's the deal with the A/C? Searchlight's on his way, dammit!

COOPER. Ask the Colonel. We have nothing to do with it.

AGENT. Cut some pineapple, why don't you?

COOPER. He happens to love it.

AGENT. Yeah? Well, you better not let his tongue bleed this time. We thought he was poisoned for crissake.

COOPER. Fine. And when he asks me for more, I'll tell him you said no.

AGENT. You better not. My job's to protect him, you know that.

COOPER. And my job's to make him comfortable.

MARY. Sounds like a stalemate, gentlemen.

AGENT [*touching his ear*]. Water been tested yet?

COOPER. Chemist just left.

AGENT. And?

COOPER. And what? I assume it was clean. Ask them.

AGENT. Is the entire plane this hot?

COOPER. I put a fan in their sitting room.

AGENT. A fan?! You idiot—all a fan does is blow the hot air around.

COOPER. Why don't you go take a bullet for somebody?

AGENT. Goddamn waitresses. [*Walks out of the galley and exits via downstage corridor.*] Rhubarb, rhubarb, rhubarb, rhubarb, rhubarb.

COOPER. Where were we?

MARY. The A/C. The plane. Why wasn't it ready?

COOPER. Ground crew got the call late.

MARY. But there was talk of him resigning for weeks.

COOPER. Nobody expected it. In six years of serving the President, not once did I see him so much as fold a hand of cards. Quitting is simply repulsive to the man.

MARY. Think we'll keep this duty with Ford?

COOPER. I don't see why not. The few times he's been aboard, the Vice President's liked me, and he loves your cooking.

MARY. Good man, I think. But not the sharpest tool in the shed.

[*The* AGENT *crosses downstage.*]

AGENT [*into sleeve*]. Rhubarb, rhubarb. Searchlight is moving. Repeat…Searchlight is moving. Rhubarb, rhubarb.

SCENE TWO

The private sitting room aboard Air Force One. There are three swivel chairs, and next to the middle chair is a small table with two phones on it: one beige, the other red. The galley counter is now a bar, with an ice bucket, glasses and decanters of liquor. A fan sits on the bar.

From time to time, the AGENT *paces the downstage corridor, looking out the plane window and standing guard outside the sitting room door. As the scene opens,* COOPER *mixes a highball. Holding the glass up, he pours in two fingers of liquor, pauses, then fills it nearly to the brim.*

COOPER. That ought to hold her. Until we take off at least.

NIXON [*offstage, booming*]. Dammit, somebody turn on the air!

[*Enter* NIXON, MRS. NIXON, *and the* AGENT; *they cross downstage.*]

NIXON. I'm dying here. Where's Coop?

AGENT. In your sitting room, I believe, Mr. President. [*Into sleeve.*] Searchlight is aboard. Repeat, Searchlight is aboard. Rhubarb, rhubarb.

[NIXON, MRS. NIXON *and the* AGENT *file into the sitting room.* COOPER *stands at attention holding the highball and a magazine.*]

NIXON. And another thing.

AGENT. Sir?

NIXON. There's a mob of reporters out there. Ask the Colonel if he can suck a few into the engines for the President.

AGENT. Yes, sir!

[*The* Agent *runs out of the sitting room and exits via the downstage corridor.*]

Cooper. Welcome aboard, Mr. President. Mrs. Nixon.

Mrs. Nixon. Good to see you, Cooper. God, am I going to miss you.

[Mrs. Nixon *takes the drink and magazine, and plops into a chair.* Nixon *also sits down.* Cooper *pours another drink and hands it to* Nixon.]

Nixon. So what's the word on the air, Coop? Hotter than an Egyptian whorehouse in here.

Cooper. The Colonel says it should kick in once we're airborne, sir.

Nixon. Kick in? What kind of Puerto Rican operation is this?

Mrs. Nixon [*pointing at ceiling*]. Uh-uh, Richard. Remember…

Nixon. Oh, to hell with it. They already got me. Now there's loyalty for you, Coop. Appoint a man Chief Justice and the sonovabitch rules against you when you really need him. [*To* Mrs. Nixon.] I'll tell you one thing, Pat, he's never setting foot in Casa Pacifica.

Mrs. Nixon. I'm sure that won't be an issue.

Nixon. Last flight and the damn air isn't working. I tell you, the Big Guy's just got it in for me. Goddamn hell of a week. Hell of a week.

[Mrs. Nixon *jingles her ice for a refill.* Cooper *walks over with a decanter of liquor.*]

Mrs. Nixon. I told him the blue suit was too heavy. I suggested the linen. But does he listen to me, Cooper? Nooooo…

Nixon. You can't resign the Presidency wearing linen. For crissake, I'm not going out looking like George Plimpton. Red, white and blue—that's what you wear. Hell, Jack Kennedy wouldn't have worn the linen.

Mrs. Nixon. Jack Kennedy wouldn't have had to resign.

Nixon. Bah, the hell with you. Am I right or am I right, Coop?

Cooper. I think you both have valid points. Your suit is rather heavy, though. What is it, sir—wool?

Nixon. No…it's a blend. [*Loosens his tie.*] By God, it's hot. Coop, go get the Colonel. I want to talk to him. And take my jacket.

Cooper. Yes, Mr. President.

[Cooper *exits.* Nixon *checks his watch and pats the beige phone.*]

Nixon. You know, Pat, I've still got a while before they give Gerry the show. How about I call Schlesinger and get Coop a promotion? He's earned it, hasn't he?

Mrs. Nixon. If he keeps my drink refilled, I'd be inclined to agree.

NIXON. Gerry's probably rifling through the desk by now, looking for souvenirs.

MRS. NIXON. I should think he's rehearsing his speech. Did you get to see it?

NIXON. No. Claimed his guys hadn't written anything yet. God knows what he'll say. Just hope he doesn't welsh on our little deal.

MRS. NIXON. The pardon?

NIXON [*shaking his fist*]. Come on, Gerry! Don't let me down!

MRS. NIXON. Who's delivering your letter to Henry?

NIXON. Haig. That is, if the SOB doesn't anoint himself on the way over to Foggy Bottom.

[COOPER *and the* PILOT *cross downstage and enter the sitting room.*]

PILOT. You wanted to see me, Mr. President?

NIXON. Yes, Colonel. The air. Tell me this isn't some conspiracy to make my last flight a living hell.

PILOT. No, sir. This has happened a couple times before. Far as I can tell, the A/C needs the jolt we get at takeoff. A little glitch, sir, but she should kick in. I'm ninety percent certain.

NIXON. Ninety percent's not good enough, Colonel. I'm still the President here, and I want air conditioning!

[NIXON *slams his fist down. They all prick up their ears.*
NIXON *raises his hand to a vent.*]

COOPER. I can't believe it, sir, but it seems you fixed it.
Good work, Mr. President!

NIXON. Well, at least the plane knows who's still in
charge. Let's get moving, Colonel. Before those vultures outside try to make hay out of our sitting here.

PILOT. Of course, Mr. President.

NIXON. And clip a few of them if you can.

PILOT. I think they're well off the runway, sir, but I'll try.

NIXON. Good man.

[*The* PILOT *exits.* MRS. NIXON *jingles her glass.* COOPER
refills it.]

COOPER. Mr. President, ma'am—I need you to strap in
now. I'll drop in again as soon as we level off.

NIXON. Stick around, Coop. No need to be so formal.
Last time we'll get to see you.

COOPER. Okay, sir.

[COOPER *sits in the third chair and buckles up.*]

NIXON. How's your daughter, Coop? What is she now…
eleven, twelve?

COOPER. Twenty, sir.

NIXON. My God, but they grow up fast. Seems like just yesterday when I walked Tricia down the aisle. By the way, Coop, when was your last promotion?

COOPER. Oh, I don't know. Three years ago maybe. Why, sir?

NIXON. The clock hasn't run out on Dick Nixon yet. [*He picks up the beige phone handset.*] Get me Jim at the Pentagon....Well, I don't care if he's in a john someplace. Put him on the line....All right. Tell him the President called from Air Force One....No, President Nixon. Tell him to call me back before the handoff, understood?...Thank you....Mrs. Nixon and I appreciate your support. [*He hangs up the telephone.*] He'll call back. They're buzzing around down there, trying to be first in line to kiss Gerry's ass.

PILOT [*offstage, as over a PA*]. Good morning. We've reached our cruising altitude of 35,000 feet. It's now safe to get up and move around the cabin. Enjoy the flight.

COOPER. Mr. President, please don't spend your final hours trying to finagle a promotion for me.

NIXON. Finagle? No need to do that, son. I'm still the President.

COOPER. Of course, sir.

NIXON [*to MRS. NIXON*]. Where's my briefcase?

MRS. NIXON. The football? You're upset, Richard. Probably not a good idea to play with the launch codes right now.

NIXON. Not the damn football. My briefcase! Don't I have any work to do? Papers to sign? Anything?

MRS. NIXON. Sit back and relax for once, Richard. Coop, what's for lunch?

NIXON. I'll find out.

[*He reaches for the beige phone and mistakenly picks up the red phone handset instead.*]

NIXON. Send Mary in, please.

MRS. NIXON. Richard!

NIXON [*mortified*]. Oh, Mr. Chairman?...Yes, this is the President. Sorry, picked up the wrong phone....Good. Yes, I'm on my way home now....No, not quite exile. Southern California is hardly Siberia. Political Siberia maybe, but at least it's warm....Say, you wouldn't happen to know what my chef is serving onboard today, would you? [*He laughs.*] Very good, Mr. Chairman. And you, too. Goodbye. [*He hangs up.*] Boy, good thing Leo's got a sense of humor. [*He picks up the beige phone this time.*] Please send Mary in. Thanks. [*He hangs up the telephone.*]

MRS. NIXON [*jingles the ice in her glass*]. Cooper?

COOPER. Yes, ma'am.

[*The* AGENT *crosses downstage in front of the sitting room, talking into his sleeve.*]

AGENT. Rhubarb, rhubarb, rhubarb, rhubarb.

NIXON. Agent!

AGENT [*stops, enters sitting room*]. Yes, sir?

NIXON. *Why* in holy hell do you keep saying "rhubarb"?

AGENT. It's what extras say, Mr. President. That and 'watermelon' or 'peas and carrots.' The damn playwright didn't even give me a name. He clearly favors you three, so saying "rhubarb" in places where he doesn't give me a line is an easy way to spite him. If it bothers you, sir, I'll stop.

NIXON. Damn playwrights. Glad we kept an eye on them. Make no mistake, that Tennessee Williams is a threat! Carry on, son. By all means, carry on.

AGENT. Thank you, sir! [*Walking offstage.*] Rhubarb, rhubarb, watermelon. Peas and carrots, carrots and peas.

[*The* AGENT *exits.* MARY *enters, crosses downstage and goes into the sitting room.*]

NIXON. Mary! What culinary delights do you have for your Commander in Chief today?

MARY. Mr. President, ma'am—I have all your favorites. Cold Virginia ham, hot rolls with butter, creamed asparagus and the biggest bowl of fresh pineapple you ever seen, sir.

NIXON. Can't believe how hungry I am. Anytime, Mary, anytime.

MARY. You've had a tough day already, sir. And a tough Presidency, if I may say so.

NIXON. Thank you, Mary. Bring on the lunch.

[MARY *exits.* COOPER *ties a plastic bib around the President's neck.*]

MRS. NIXON. Cooper, the M&M's—the ones with the President's seal? Fill a suitcase with them.

NIXON. Smart thinking, Pat. They're swell little gifts. Guests come to Casa Pacifica, we can still give 'em a little piece of the White House.

COOPER. I don't know how many we have aboard, but I'll round up as many as I can.

MRS. NIXON. And some of the coasters.

COOPER. Yes, ma'am.

[*The* AGENT *runs across downstage and enters the sitting room panting.*]

NIXON. Agent! What's wrong?

AGENT [*breathless*]. Mr. President, we might…have a fire…in the Dungeon. There's smoke coming…out of there.

NIXON. Dungeon? I didn't authorize any prisoners on this plane.

COOPER. No, Mr. President. The Dungeon is what we call the crawl space under this floor. It's between here and the hold, sir.

AGENT. Mr. President, I have to advise the pilot so he can make an emergency landing.

NIXON [*jumps out of chair, tears off bib*]. Absolutely not. We're not landing anything, understand me? We're fixing this—right now! Jesus Christ…this is just the metaphor my Presidency needs—Air Force One going down in flames.

AGENT. Mr. President, I can't allow it.

NIXON [*rolls up his shirt sleeves*]. I don't care. Get a fire extinguisher, you're coming along. Now, Coop…take me to this Dungeon.

———◆•◆•◆———

SCENE THREE

An empty stage. NIXON, COOPER *and the* AGENT *inch across the floor on their bellies.* NIXON *and* COOPER *are crawling face-forward; the* AGENT *crawls backward waving a gun around, covering their rear.* COOPER *shines a flashlight ahead of them while* NIXON *drags a large red fire extinguisher.*

NIXON. See anything yet?

COOPER. Just smoke, sir.

NIXON. No flames?

COOPER. No flames.

NIXON. Shine it over there. No, the other way. There. That look like anything to you?

COOPER. A wire, sir. A lot of wires, actually.

NIXON. Some of them seem to be smoldering, Cooper.

COOPER. I think we should leave them alone, Mr. President.

AGENT [*whining*]. What's going on? It's hard crawling backwards like this, Mr. President. I can't see anything.

NIXON. Just keep covering our rear, son. You're doing great. Coop, get the light on this. Never used one of these before. First time for everything, I suppose. [*Reads extinguisher label.*] Instructions. One. Pull pin. Coop, where the hell's the pin on this thing?

COOPER. It's usually a little metal ring. Stick your finger in and yank it out.

NIXON. Ah, got it. Two. Start back six feet. Are we back six feet?

COOPER. Mmm, maybe five, Mr. President.

NIXON. Screw it, close enough. Three. Aim at base. Base? Base of what?

COOPER. The flames, sir.

NIXON. There are no flames.

COOPER. Base of the smoke then.

NIXON. But why the base? Seems to me you'd want to hit it right on the flames.

COOPER. I don't know, sir.

NIXON. *Base.* Whoever makes these things, I hope Edgar's bugging their bedrooms, the stupid bastards. [*Reading the extinguisher label again.*] Squeeze lever—hmm, more of a trigger, really—and sweep side to side. All right, Coop. Ready?

COOPER. Go for it, Mr. President.

[NIXON *sprays the extinguisher. It wobbles in his hands and sprays wildly. Finally he focuses the plume on one spot and yells as he sprays.*]

NIXON. Get some, you sonovabitch! Get some, Burger! Get some, McGovern! Get some, Jane Fonda! All of you Commies—get some, get some, get some!

COOPER. Get some *what*, sir?

[NIXON *stops spraying. He is out of breath.*]

NIXON. Is it out, Coop? Put the light on it.

COOPER. I don't see any smoke, sir.

NIXON. Ow! Why's the extinguisher so cold?

COOPER. Chemical reaction, sir. Endothermic, I believe.

NIXON. How the hell do you know that?

COOPER. I don't know, sir.

NIXON [*checking his watch*]. Yup, still in charge.

[*He raises his fist victoriously.*]

COOPER. Very good, sir. How about lunch?

NIXON. Right. Agent Noname? We're backing up now.

AGENT. Okay, Mr. President. [*He crawls offstage.*] Rhubarb, rhubarb, rhubarb.

NIXON. Wait a second, Coop. Get the light on this. Good.

COOPER. What is it, Mr. President?

NIXON. Made in China, Coop. Made in China. You heard Dick Nixon say it first: someday those crafty sons-of-bitches are going to make everything. And they'll raze every village and starve every grandmother to do it, believe me.

COOPER. That's bleak, sir.

NIXON. No, you know what's bleak?

COOPER. What's that, sir?

NIXON. Knowing you were the most powerful man on Earth, that you'll be out of a job in less than an hour, and that the totality of what you do for the rest of your life won't match the good you could do with one decision as President. That, Coop, is bleak.

COOPER. Sir, I stand corrected.

NIXON. It's not that I was loyal to a bunch of shits who didn't deserve it. Like Socrates said, "Virtue is its own reward." You know what really bothers me?

COOPER. What's that, sir?

NIXON. Those two on the Washington Post. I mean, to be brought down by a couple of longhairs. For crissake, boys, put on a clean shirt once in a while, will you? I saw the surveillance photos. The underarm sweat stains, both of them! It's disgusting. If the liberals were going to bring me down, I wish it'd been those vultures at the Times. Say what you want about their politics, those are some well-dressed reporters. Sharp, every one of them.

COOPER. Sir, we really should get out of here. There's still a lot of smoke.

NIXON. Okay, Coop. Lead the way.

⸻⸻◆⸻⸻

SCENE FOUR

The sitting room. NIXON and MRS. NIXON are seated with trays on their laps. COOPER and MARY stand on either side of the room.

NIXON. Mary, you outdid yourself. One of the best meals I've had. Made this day a lot easier to bear.

MARY. I'm touched, Mr. President. Thank you.

NIXON. Probably our adventure in the Dungeon, right, Coop? Got my appetite up.

COOPER. Absolutely, sir.

[COOPER *takes their trays and hands them to* MARY, *who exits.*]

NIXON. So what now, Coop? Got a long flight ahead of us. I need a challenge. How about we break out the Scrabble?

COOPER. Sounds good, sir.

[*A phone RINGS.* MRS. NIXON *sips her highball and flips through her magazine.*]

MRS. NIXON. Phone, Richard. The *beige* one this time.

NIXON. On it. [*Picks up the phone.*] Hello, Jim?...Oh....I see....And nobody can find him?...Ah....And you checked the Sit Room, of course....Right. Well, make sure he gets the following message: Cooper Jones, the Chief Flight Steward aboard Air Force One, is to be promoted immediately. Got it?...Okay. [*He hangs up.*] Coop, get me paper and a pencil, would you?

COOPER. Here you go, sir.

[NIXON *scribbles on the paper, mumbling to himself as he writes, then tears off the page and hands it to* COOPER.]

NIXON. In case Jim—the Secretary of Defense—doesn't get the message.

COOPER. Thank you, Mr. President. I'll go get the Scrabble board.

NIXON. Very good. Prepare to be routed, young man.

[COOPER *exits.* NIXON *is seen swiveling in the chair, gripping the armrests, glancing around the room, clearly beside himself with inaction. He glances at his watch and puts his face in his hands.*]

PILOT [*offstage, over PA*]. Kansas City, this is former Air Force One. Please change our call sign to Sierra-Alpha-Mike Two-Seven-Zero-Zero-Zero. Over.

THE END

ABOUT THE AUTHOR

Chris Orcutt has written professionally for 25 years as a novelist, short story writer, journalist, scriptwriter, speechwriter and playwright. He has also taught high school U.S. history and college writing.

He is the creator of the critically acclaimed Dakota Stevens Mystery Series, including *A Real Piece of Work* (#1), *The Rich Are Different* (#2), *A Truth Stranger Than Fiction* (#3), and *The Perfect Triple Threat* (#4). For information on future installments and his other writing, visit his website (below).

Orcutt's short story collection, *The Man, The Myth, The Legend*, was voted by IndieReader as one of the best books of 2013. And his modern pastoral novel *One Hundred Miles from Manhattan* (an IndieReader Best Book for 2014) prompted *Kirkus Reviews* to favorably compare Orcutt to Pulitzer Prize-winning author John Cheever.

His short fiction has been published in *Potomac Review* and other literary journals. It has also won a few modest awards, most notably 55 Fiction's World's Shortest Stories. As a newspaper reporter he received a New York Press Association award. *The Ronald And Other Plays* is his first collection of plays.

If you would like to contact Chris, you can email him at corcutt007@yahoo.com. For more information about Chris and his writing, or to follow his blog, visit his website: www.orcutt.net.

Excerpt from
One Hundred Miles from Manhattan

One Hundred Miles from Manhattan is a novel about an upscale rural community (Wellington, NY), where the hills and the seemingly quaint village conceal lives of love, lust, adultery, tragedy and small wars. Following is the opening of *One Hundred Miles from Manhattan*.

Until that early June evening in bed beside her much older husband, Caprice Highgate had never heard the screams of terrified cows. In fact, before moving upstate from Manhattan to Wellington she hadn't heard so much as a *moo* out of one. Even after three years, on nights like this she longed for the white noise of the city. The sustained silence of the country was deafening, and when there *was* noise, like now with the wailing cows and the howling coyotes, it more than startled her—it shredded her nerves. She waved a hand at the open windows.

"I wish you'd do something about that."

Hamilton was reading an armchair safari book: Robert Ruark's *Use Enough Gun.* He turned a page. Caprice glanced at the double-barreled shotgun hanging over the bedroom door.

"Maybe try *using* a gun instead of reading about them," she said. "Did you hear me?"

"What?"

"Your cows. There are coyotes out there, Hamilton. Hear them?"

"Coyotes?"

"Well, they're not wolves."

"Stephen's on top of it, I'm sure," he said. "Take a pill."

"That's your answer—take a pill."

"Caprice, don't be melodramatic."

She put on her robe and went downstairs.

She poured herself a glass of wine, padded into the great room, opened the French doors and sat in an armchair facing outside. For a minute it was pin-quiet, but then another burst of the melee shattered the silence: the calves' bleats for help, followed by the coyotes' eerie whistles. She sipped some wine and gazed out into the darkness. Half a mile away, Celia's bedroom lights glared across the long, narrow pond (a moat, really) in front of the mansion. Caprice wondered how the first Mrs. Highgate was faring and whether the carnage was keeping her awake, too. She hoped so. She hoped the bitch died from sleep deprivation so she and Hamilton could move into the mansion. This place had always felt like a child's playhouse by comparison.

In the morning after coffee, Caprice dressed in riding clothes and Wellies, got in her Range Rover and drove to the stables. One of the hands must have seen her coming because when Caprice got inside, Giorgio was already out of his stall with the saddle pad on his back. The air was thick with hay dust. She sneezed.

"Bless you," the stable hand said.

"Thanks. Stephen around?"

"Office, Miss Caprice."

She changed into her riding boots, grabbed her crop and helmet, and marched into the office. Stephen was on the phone. He raised a finger to her.

Caprice stood at the window and pretended to watch Giorgio being walked out to the yard. Instead, in the reflection she watched Stephen trace the curve of her backside. Caprice knew her ass was good, but the breeches helped.

"Miss Caprice," Stephen said, hanging up the phone. "What can I do you for?"

She fastened her helmet strap. "Have you *heard* the cows at night, Stephen?"

"Heard what?"

"You're as bad as Hamilton. Don't tell me you haven't noticed. The cows, the coyotes."

"Coyotes? *No*…they're not big enough to go after cattle."

She stared at him. "So you think I'm hearing things."

"No, it's just—"

"Saddle up, Stephen. We're going riding."

"Where?"

"Wherever the cows are."

He leaned back in his chair. "That won't be so easy, Miss Caprice."

Stephen launched into a monologue about Hamilton's 200 head of cattle being spread across all 2,500 acres of the estate. Since the animals wandered freely spring through fall, the noises Caprice heard—*if* she'd heard them—could have come from anywhere. As the estate manager, he knew about these things.

"Humor me then," she said.

"You're the boss." Stephen grabbed a rifle from behind his chair.

"What's that for?"

"In case you're right."

They rode all morning, scouring patchworks of fields separated by dense hedgerows. The weather was clear, affording a beautiful view of the Village of Wellington and the endlessly undulating, tree-dappled hills. They also saw a lot of Hamilton's cattle—Black Angus, Stephen informed her—as they searched for signs of the violence that had kept her awake last night.

As the noon fire horn carried faintly from the village, Stephen pulled up beneath the ancient oak that sheltered the Highgate family cemetery. The earliest stone dated back to 1711. Tiger lilies grew wild along the picket fence. Caprice loathed coming to this spot on the estate; headstones awaited Hamilton and Celia, but there was no space earmarked for her.

"Why are we stopping here?" she asked.

Stephen patted his horse's neck. "This is the last field the ruckus could've come from."

"What about Celia's side of the estate?"

"Sound wouldn't carry all that way."

"But we just heard the fire horn."

"Course we did. That's super loud."

"Wait a second." Caprice shifted in her saddle. "Isn't it possible you're simply inured to these noises—growing up in the country and all?"

"*Inured?*"

"Used to."

"Maybe. It's just…I've got a lot of work back at the office, you know? And don't you have that big party this weekend?"

She heaved out a "Yes," not because there was a lot left to do, but because Hamilton's turning 70 raised a recurring question for her: namely, what was she doing with a man over twice her age? Until recently, she had told herself the wealthy aged better than other people. But that was before he began to lose his hearing, a condition that dramatically highlighted the difference in their ages.

"We should probably get back, huh?" Stephen said.

Caprice nudged Giorgio into a trot and was practicing her post when Stephen called out behind her.

"I say, Miss Caprice…you've become one heck of an equestrienne. Yessir, you sure can sit a horse."

Of course she could. When a person had as much free time as she, with nothing to do but plan parties and serve on bullshit committees, and a modicum of self-discipline to take a riding lesson every other day, she damn well better be good at it. And then Caprice had a realization that made her feel hollow: *riding was the only thing that gave her life purpose.* How she had arrived at her current situation was suddenly a mystery to her. She was the second lady of the manor on Wellington's oldest and wealthiest estate. She had more money in her personal bank account than she'd made in a decade as a fashion writer. And she straddled her very own and very expensive thoroughbred. But she couldn't remember how any of this had come to be. It was as though she'd been in suspended animation for the past three years and had only now awakened.

"Goodbye, Stephen."

She trotted away. Then, flashing Giorgio the whip, she clutched his mane as he broke into a gallop, and together they jumped the fence at the end of the field....